DATE DUE

CÉZANNE

Portrait of the artist. Drawing. 1890-95.

Gilles Plazy

CÉZANNE

CRESCENT BOOKS
NEW YORK

Translated from the French by *Carol Lee Rathman*

This 1990 edition published by Crescent Books,
distributed by Crown Publishers, Inc., 225 Park Avenue South,
New York, New York 10003.

Printed and bound: in Italy

ISBN 0-517-694824

h g f e d c b a

Table of contents

Index of illustrations

Mountains in Provence. 1878-80.
Cardiff, National Museum of Wales

INTRODUCTION

Cézanne spoke an artistic language that goes beyond the plain and simple painted image, a secret language that underlies his images and injects them with a life of their own. But the question immediately arises: Is it possible to understand the lessons of this old painter, a recluse in his beloved mountains, without having walked those same slopes; is it possible to interpret the messages he hid in his canvases without having first learned the language he used?

Cézanne as the unquestionable father, the founder of a modern art – this is the truism that we must evaluate. But first in order to find out more about him then the biography that has been a thousand times repeated, the limits put up by art history must be overcome.

In our study of Cézanne we must not be tempted to follow those who, hungry for more personal information about the man, ignore his painting. Bearing in mind that Cézanne resolutely clung to his privacy, the fact that he continuously effaced his works may convince us that they are the key to his secrets: the artist's work was his *raison d'être*; he and his paintings were one. If we wish to know more about the man, we must look more closely at his work.

The work of the mature Cézanne, who had progressed far along the road he had set out upon, a road with no final goal to mark its end, makes a lasting impression. But now we must look at it as if for the first time, stripped of our pre-conceptions and outside of any historical context – a context from which, perhaps more than anything else, Cézanne sought to free himself. Look at it and contemplate it; rather than putting words to it, we must absorb its radiance, breathe in its meaning.

In painting, it is the eye that reasons; the eye of the artist meets that of the spectator. In the best of cases, when the spectator turns his gaze back to the world, he sees it with new eyes. Cézanne's identity merged with that of his subjects. He studied his subjects in a hundred different ways; he consumed himself in his dialogue with the still life, and above all he

Aix Landscape. 1877.

ceaselessly examined the landscape, his landscape.

He did not have a restless paintbrush; he felt no urge to paint new subjects. A single plot of land served his purposes. A magnificent mountain, Sainte-Victoire, alone offered more than enough mystery for his imagination.

Cézanne lived in the solitude of Aix, his few friends far away, with the still-alive memory of the master painters he had so admired at the Louvre, and the companionship of the poets Virgil and Lucretius. His proud old age was dedicated entirely to painting, embedded in his destiny: finally, the man became one with his painting, the painter triumphed, wielding his brush to his very last days – apotheosis!

With a man as religious as Cézanne, we need not hesitate to call such devotion to painting mystical. Painting for him was just a means to penetrate the secrets of the world and to communicate with God. This communication requires from the beginning a shedding of the layers of consciousness to arrive at the truth within. This alone was what permitted him finally to resolve the contradictions that arose in his lifetime of work: in the works of his old age, he transcended the romantic passion of his youth and the yearning to get back to the classicism of his maturity. This is an achievement that only the very short-sighted could reduce to the introduction of the cube, the cone and the sphere into Western painting.

He left but a few examples of this geometrical style and most of his efforts were concentrated on the luminous aura he gave to the world, with which he wed volumes to volumes and he unified space. Cézanne's use of light was the divine grace that transported the evanescence of the Impressionists to the plane of eternity. It never appears in Bracque and Picasso's Cubism, as they pursued only his research of form. Neither artist was to be Cézanne's heir (and it would be quite mistaken to trace the roots of abstract art through Cubism to him).

What remains is an outstanding beauty that is recognised today. And an especially enduring qual-ity of his work is this dialogue with the earth, best represented by a mountain, an appeal to God in terms of real things. The task of the mystic is to work towards a reconciliation between man and God. There are two approaches to this end: one considers the earth as the site of man's fall, and consequently rejects it; the other worships the earth as the site where God walked – and the entire history of Christianity alternates between these two conceptions.

Cézanne sought in all of his canvases to depict the harmony of the earth, to invent a painting style that could reflect this harmony. This is why he looked to values inherent in painting and broke away from the narrative tendency in art. The Impressionists merely passed from an epic narrative to a more realistic style; Cézanne burst forth in a celebration. And in this way, after Cézanne, art was never the same.

PORTRAIT OF THE ARTIST
AS A PAINTER

One wonders how this young man of Aix, son of a milliner-become-banker with a keen business sense, was introduced to painting. How a vocation comes to be is always a mystery, and the young Paul Cézanne did not discover his as early as might be thought. Indeed, his father had envisioned quite a different future for his only son: he had hoped to turn his experience as a self-made businessman to his son's advantage, and he had hoped for his son to be a worthy successor. In truth, Paul did profit from his father's success, for though he did pass through some hard times, this is what permitted him to dedicate himself to painting without cares about earning a living.

Louis-Auguste Cézanne learned the millinery craft in Paris and from there went to Aix to open his shop. (He had grown up in a nearby village). Times were not always easy. He wanted to make his fortune, to succeed, and eventually he did. It was not until he was forty years old that he took a young woman fifteen years his junior as his mistress. She bore him two children before they were married: Paul was the first, born in 1839, his sister Marie came two years later.

The milliner Cézanne quickly discovered the advantages of credit. Business was going strong and he lived modestly; if others needed cash why not lend it to them in return for a little interest? This plan worked so well that when the bank of Aix folded, it was easy for him to form a partnership with the old cashier and take it over. the bourgeoisie of Aix might have found something of dubious morality in this success story, but the Cézanne family's road to fortune no longer presented any obstacles.

During this time, the young Paul was growing up. His was a difficult, brooding, passionate, sensitive character. He became a docile, shy, obedient, impressionable but good student. There is an anecdote about him that testifies to his precocious genius; it is apparently true, but perhaps not all that meaningful, because children often demon-

Study of a Negro model. 1860-65.　　　　　　*Study of a standing nude.* 1860-65.

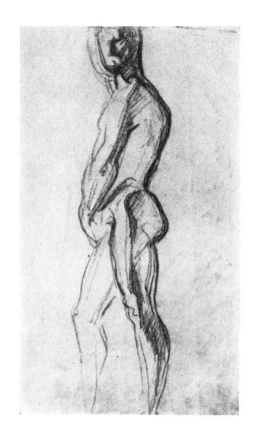

Chestnut Trees at the Jas de Bouffan.
Minneapolis, Minneapolis Institute of Art.

The Mill on the Coulouse.
Berlin, National Galerie.

Manet. *Café Guerbois.*
Cambridge (Mass.), Fogg Museum of Art.

Van Gogh. *Portrait of Père Tanguy.*
Private collection.

Portrait of Achille Emperaire.
Paris, Louvre.

Manet. *Portrait of Zola.*
Paris, Louvre.

Portrait of the Artist's Father Reading L'Evènement.
Private collection.

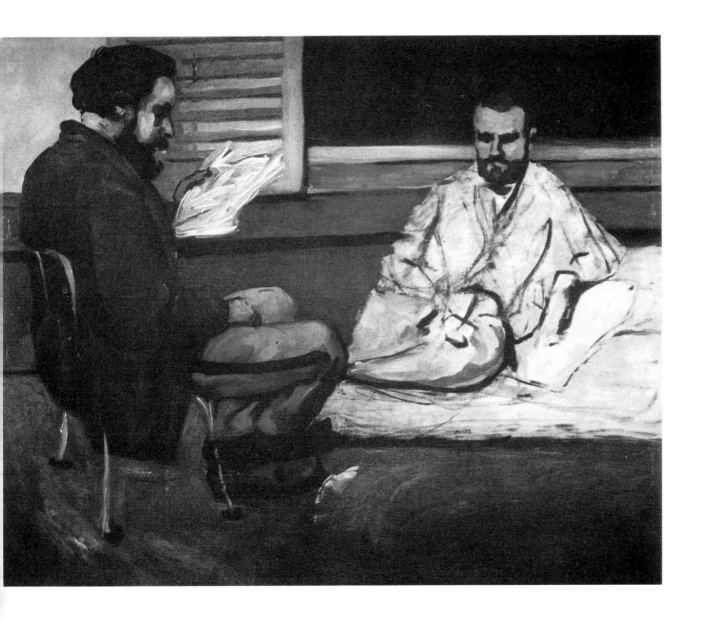

strate natural talent. One day little Paul Cézanne scrawled a charcoal sketch of a famous monument of Aix, the Pont de Mirabeau, on the wall of a building. Passing by, one of Paul's father's friends was truly astonished by the child's skill. Madame Cézanne, who was a bit more imaginative than her husband, was apparently quite proud of the sketch; perhaps from that very moment she started to harbor certain romantic and hardly banking dreams for her son, but we lack the information to say what part she played in determining her son's future.

Though he was a good student, art was not the subject in which Paul Cézanne at first excelled. His schoolmate Emile Zola, who was to become the famous writer, got much better grades in the subject. The boys shared a deep friendship and a solid alliance in net opposition to the rest of their class, which had assumed more of the bourgeois values system than they. This friendship was made fast with Zola's gift of a basket of apples to Cézanne, who had taken a beating to defend his friend!

Cézanne's adolescence unfolded in the company of Zola and a third boy, despite the somewhat closed family atmosphere.

Whenever they could, the boys ran off to explore the countryside and to invent fantastic adventures and matchless destinies for themselves. Such inventions are not unusual for boys of this age, but when one learns that they spent their childhoods roaming places like le Tholonet, le Château Noir, Bibémus quarry at the foot of the Mont Sainte-Victoire: these are precisely the names that will appear over and over again in the painter's works. He had already taken possession of the land, his native land, to which he was to remain incredibly faithful all his life. Without knowing it, he was already taking nourishment from his mother country.

Nonetheless, it was in literature and not drawing that the young Cézanne showed most promise; a passionate scholar, he would not let the younger Zola get the better of him. No, Cézanne was a good student of letters, who learned Victor Hugo's works by heart and wrote his own verse in profusion. He wanted to become a poet, as did his two friends, inspired by their idol Alfred de Musset. What led him then to enroll in the Aix school of art?

While signing up for night classes at the art school meant a minimal commitment to a young man who had the world to set on fire (he even played in a boisterous brass band!), there is nothing to make us think that he was at all decided about his calling, this enrollment was a first step towards his artistic career. He also went to a museum which exhibited some 17th-century works, including a painting attributed to Louis Nain, *The Cardplayers*. It seems that even then he showed good observational skills and a good visual memory, but it is difficult to know more than this.

What is more certain is that Cézanne threw himself into his artwork when Zola's departure for Paris left him feeling quite alone in Aix. With some difficulty he graduated form the school, and at his father's insistence began his law studies. The law failed to arouse his interest, which instead was growing stronger in the field of drawing and painting.

This was when he decided to become an artist, and Zola heartily encouraged him to speak with his father about it. Cézanne *père* was vexed by his son's infatuation and ardently hoped that law school would soon take the upper hand.

Negotiations went on for several months, but in the end Louis-Auguste gave in. He personally accompanied Paul to Paris and gave him a meagre allowance, just enough to live on. Paul left behind at the Jas de Bouffan – the family's newly-acquired country house near Aix – four panels that bear witness to his chafing passion for painting: in imitation of Ingres, with the seasons as its subject, the brushwork on the panels shows a discrete style. They are signed with bold irony, in the name of the admired – but not revered – master Ingres. In his mother's room, his copy of Frillie's *The Kiss of the Muse* at the Aix museum, attests to a certain complicity between mother and son, against the father's will. But Cézanne was then just a young artist groping for his way, plagued by doubts about ever being able to reach is goal, He knew that he wanted to paint, and that he had something to say, but he felt blocked and feared that he would never overcome this. He was sure that in Paris, working in such a dynamic environment and seeing firsthand the masterpieces housed in the Louvre, he would make progress. At this point, Cézanne's desire to paint was stronger than his confidence in his talent.

In Paris he was reunited with his friend Zola, who was sure of his future and his talent, but quite starving, and near the wonderful and imposing Louvre and the Salon, which to his small-town eyes seemed wonderful. Zola acted as his guide and showed him the way to the Académie Suisse, a haven for young painters who asked for nothing more in life than models and comrades. Delacroix and Courbet were among the greats who had gone there to work, Manet and Monet represented the younger generation who had passed through. While there, Cézanne met another artist from Aix, already quite used to city ways, and they engaged in endless discussions: these two must have hashed over art more than once, questioning the works of great masters and planning their own. He also met Pissarro here, who offered encouragement.

The intoxicating life of Paris did not go to his head. He concentrated fully on painting, but his personality did not improve, even with his friends, whose patience he tried to the breaking point. Winning over Paris and mastering his painting technique were to be a long and hard battle, and this he knew, but why should he attempt to conquer Paris when it was enough to paint? And how could he hope to achieve greatness in painting? Cézanne poured all of his efforts into a portrait of Zola. The image that he sought to paint eluded his brush and he finally, in a fit of rage, tore up the canvas. The only thing left for him to do, he thought, was to admit his failure to his father and comply with his wishes. His Parisian adventure had not lasted six months, when Paul took a job with a bank.

It was therefore in a state of deepest despair that he began his work with the accounting ledgers, brooding over his defeat and resigning himself with difficulty to what he considered his incapacity. He rediscovered the natural beauty of his beloved countryside, especially in its full autumn regalia, and basked in it whenever he could. His art came back to him; the urgency of his calling never seemed more imperative. He returned to the drawing school, and set up a studio in the Jas du Bouffan. Aix was as it should have been, the setting for the wedding celebration between Cézanne and art. This time, Cézanne's destiny was clearly set before him: he wanted to enroll in the Ecole des Beaux-Arts in Paris.

Aix-Paris: for the rest of his life, Cézanne evolved along this axis, with very few digressions. That autumn, he returned to Paris as an Artist, moved in near the Luxembourg museum and hastened to sign up for courses at the Académie Suisse. With a new sense of self-confidence he overcame his initial crippling doubts. He had triumphed over a failure that had seemed at first to condemn him to the life his father had chosen for him. He would not be the worthy successor that Louis-Auguste had hoped to find in his son. He now knew that he could no longer sidestep art. The artist that he was to become stirred inside of him. But for now he was a mere painter's pupil: a starving "bohemian" who had only his ambition. He returned to his old Parisian companions, and especially Zola, who was increasingly betraying

poetry for short-stories and novelettes which he hoped to get published in periodicals. There is no doubt that Cézanne did not have Zola's ebullient self-confidence: the painter prided himself on his searching nature, on the quest for truth that painting could offer him, but it remained for him to find this truth, if he could – he still had a great deal to learn. Zola's stength, on the other hand, lay in his determination: he had to live by his writing and he was convinced that one day he would succeed. Cézanne, at least by then, no longer doubted his vocation. He doubted only his talent, since he continually raised his sights; he ceaselessly sought to surpass himself with iron-like discipline. Zola, instead, found his writer's personality by giving free rein to his headstrong talent.

In Paris, overcoming his shyness, Cézanne eagerly took part in the atmosphere of discussion, debate, and fertile exchange with other painters. An ardent admirer of Delacroix, Cézanne was one of the group who tried to pick up the pieces of Romanticism – a movement that had not offered as much to painting as it had to poetry or to music. He saw in Delacroix a sort of god of modern painting, a "middle-road" between Ingres' pretty charm and the insipidness of the official painters. The latter dominated the Salon, the annual exhibition that could make or break a painter, in an artistic world that was not yet aware of the power of the merchants.

Cézanne was denied admission to the Ecole des Beaux-Arts. He did not apply to the Salon of 1863, knowing that he did not stand a chance. A very harsh jury guarded the Salon entrance, and neither Pissarro nor Manet gained admittance. The emperor himself decided to establish a Salon des Refusés. It is quite difficult to imagine what this un-academic exhibition was like, but we know enough from the journalistic and visitor accounts to understand that it was a healthy breath of fresh air, raising new hopes among the young artists. The jeering public and journalists had a great laugh before Manet's *Le Bain* (which later became famous as *Le Déjeuner sur l'herbe*), but Cézanne was full of admiration. His outspoken enthusiasm attracted attention. Cézanne, the *artiste!* His appearance was untidy, but calculated to shock, and he let his hair grow. This look was then a good deal more original than it is now. Manet was added to his list of revered masters, along with Delacroix and Courbet. Cézanne's circle of friends included Pissarro (whose friendship proved very valuable) and Bazille, as well as Renoir and Sisley. Seen from afar, in historical perspective, the bohemian lifestyle takes on a romantic glow, but then it meant facing hunger and the cold.

Meanwhile, Zola was gaining ground. He won over the laundress whom Cézanne had been chastely courting with loving glances, and became an art critic, a champion of what was not yet called the "avant-garde." He made a name for himself with his *La Confession de Claude* and earned his keep with the publication of a few literary articles. He held weekly *Soirées*. Cézanne grumbled and made no effort to socialize. Zola offered his support in the name of their old friendship, but was losing faith in the young painter's talent. It was Cézanne's own fault, thought the writer, if he did not succeed right away. In truth, Zola had become an art critic more because of his zest for ideological squabbling than for a real love of art, about which it appears he did not understand a great deal. His love of intrigue gave him insight as to whom the greybeards were and led him to promote non-conformist youths against the conservatism of the Second Empire.

Cézanne was refused by the Salon, and in truth he had been more bent on provoking than seducing them. He could be seen accompanied by his friends, carrying his canvases by handcart to exhibit them amid the jeers of the official artists. In 1866 Manet and Renoir were also rejected:

he was, then, in good company. Alas! even the Salon des Refusés was rejected, due to the uproar it had caused in its first edition. Cézanne drew up a petition for its reinstatement addressed to the minister, but received no answer; at this point he must have realized that he had nothing to expect from the institutions that controlled art.

Cézanne poured all of his energy into his future as a painter, and nothing could distract him, not even the Café Guerbois, where Manet held court among young painters. Cézanne aspired to become neither Parisian nor worldly; he relentlessly held his course.

Now, though he seemed more determined than ever, he also showed less bitterness and perhaps more patience. He had met the woman, a model named Hortense, who was to be his companion for life. He turned to the sea as his subject, painting visions of peace and harmony, which still transpired his original passion. His fervor subsided only gradually, leaving him to grapple with two fundamental forces in conflict: a romantic passion and a yearning for order. He felt that it was his destiny to make order of chaos. It was certain, in any case, that his destiny lay in painting, and nothing could take its place in his life – it was a constant, but one that he constantly renewed. Not even Hortense could come near – this new love who had managed to gain the confidence of the shy young man terrified of women and intolerant of the least physical contact, so much so that a light caress threw him into a rage. Nevertheless, she remained his companion for life, and bore him a son. Always sumbissive to the artist's prodigious egoism, she often had the patience to pose for this most dictatorial of portraitists. Cézanne kept their relationship a secret from his father for a number of years.

After the fall of the Paris Commune, Cézanne returned to Paris with Hortense. But he did not seek out the company of the artists who gradually picked up where they had left off at the Café Guerbois. He recognized his son's legitimacy, but lived alone in a lodging that overlooked the Halle aux Vins, sometimes sharing it with Achille Emperaire. He ignored the Salon, which the new Republic had failed to modernize. His good-hearted friend Pissarro bailed him out of this difficult situation by inviting him and his small family to stay in Pontoise, and by encouraging the painter to brighten his palette and to break loose from his ego in order to get closer to nature. Not much later, Cézanne settled in Auvers at the invitation of Dr. Gachet, one of the key figures in art at that time. There, he refined his painting and in his rejection of romantic excess, he achieved a new fullness. And, better, miracle of miracles! Gachet bought a few canvases from him. Perruchot reports that Cézanne, quite vexed by Gachet's gushing enthusiasm over Manet's *Olympia*, spontaneously painted a copy of his own *Modern Olympia*, done three years earlier. The doctor, who was also an artist, suggested that he try engraving, but Cézanne never drew any satisfaction from this technique.

It was also thanks to Pissarro that Cézanne came into contact with his first "dealer" the renown *père* Tanguy, the color merchant of Montmartre who gave artists paints in exchange for their canvases – which he rarely succeeded in selling. The merchant associated the luminous painting of the avant-garde which had been rejected by the Salon with the Revolution.

Upon his return to Paris, Cézanne found new grounds for hope, since Monet, Degas and Pissarro had launched a project to organize a counter-Salon. After much discussion (which went on through the first months of 1874), the exhibition of the Société Anonyme was inaugurated on 15 April, in the atelier of the photographer Nadar in Boulevard des Capucines. The Société was a cooperative of artists, painters, sculptors and engravers. Manet had declined to join it, preferring the loftier road of the Salon, in

Manet. *Olympia.*
Paris, Louvre.

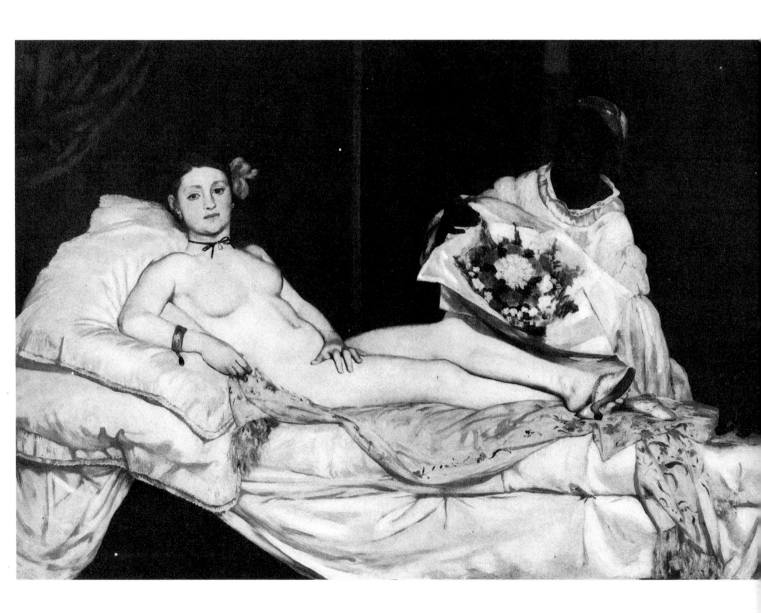

La Maison du Pendu. 1874.
Paris, Louvre.

La Maison du Pendu (detail).

Madame Cézanne in the Green House. 1890.
Private collection.

Portrait of Gustave Geffroy.
Private collection.

Portrait of Valabrègue. 1866.
Private collection.

Louis-Auguste Cézanne.
London, National Gallery.

Renoir. *Portrait of Victor Chocquet.*
Cambridge (Mass.), Fogg Museum of Art.

Renoir. *Portrait of Durand-Ruel.*
Private collection.

Portrait of Victor Chocquet. 1877.
Columbus (Ohio), Columbus Gallery of Fine Art.

The Seine. 1880.
Hamburg, Kunsthalle.

Forest Scene. 1865-68.
Private collection.

L'Estaque. 1885.
Lord Butler Collection.

43

The Bridge on the Marne.

45

whose graces he had finally fallen. He refused to associate himself with the likes of Cézanne, whom he called a "bricklayer who paints with his trowel".

It was a scandal. The critics reserved their harshest comments for those who were called the intransigéants: madmen, the mentally ill, whom an editor of *Charivari* dubbed with a name that later enjoyed great success – the Impressionists. The inspiration came from Monet's painting *Impression: Rising Sun.* But Cézanne at least experienced the joy – and the benefits – of selling a painting, his *La Maison du Pendu.* All the same, he was furious about the reactions to the exhibition and the insults he had had to endure. He fled to Aix, leaving behind in Paris his Hortense and little Paul – whose existence he had not yet had the courage to confess to his father. Under the influence of Pissarro, he had discovered the naturalist sensibilities of the Impressionists, but, never sure of himself, he still felt far from attaining his goal. One thing he was sure of was that he was on the right path: he had only to work. When he returned to Paris some months later, he was stronger, seeking through deep reflection the direction in which the Impressionist revolution was to be driven. He ignored his friends' efforts to continue their struggle as a group, even though they had organized an auction at the hotel Drouot. This would have been a complete fiasco had it not brought a new champion into their camp, a modest but passionate collector who was mad about Delacroix and became infatuated with Cézanne, thanks again to Pissarro for having introduced him to *père* Tanguy.

As his artistic studies progressed deeper and deeper, the artist, who was nearing 35 years of age, drew notice for his social maladjustment and his bohemian outlook to life. Poor, hard pressed to meet his familial responsibilities, shaken by intense waves of doubt, he even betrayed his friends, and did not participate in the exhibition they had organized at the Duran-Ruel gallery in 1876. He remained totally faithful to Aix and L'Estaque, struggling endlessly with the sun, the sea and the trees in his painting. Time was also a problem for him; when he wished, he could work with great dexterity, but now it took him months to complete a painting, to extract from a time-consuming analytical process the painted effect that he sought. In 1878 an Impressionist (from its very coinage, the group had turned this name to their advantage) exhibition was organized by Caillebotte, a great collector who had devoted himself entirely to the cause of this new trend in art. Cézanne participated in it with grand style, presenting fifteen works that he had carefully selected as representative of his work. The public reaction to the exhibition was not as hostile as in the past, but the press had still not curbed its irony.

Cézanne was the press's prime target, though Victor Chocquet – whose portrait by Cézanne had been the subject of particularly harsh criticism – rose unstintingly to the artist's defense, and one of the most insightful critics, Georges Rivière, had written, "M. Cézanne is not only a painter, he is a great painter."

It did not take long for Cézanne to realize that his cause was no longer that of the Impressionists; where they were satisfied with dissolving their subjects in a bath of light, he sought to go one step further, to restore volume to his canvases. His aim was to blend light and matter; it was the complex relationship between light and volume that interested him. Emotion no longer satisfied him. He wished to construct, to compose, that is to echo the unity of nature with the unity of painting. A friendship developed between Cézanne and another art lover, a young member of the Parisian bourgeoisie, an art collector and painter, Paul Gauguin. Gauguin was stricken with admiration for Cézanne, and later was to make further developments on the Impressionist use of color.

The intensity of Cézanne's quest did not abate. His entire life was dedidcated to painting; it alone imparted a meaning to his life. His marriage weighed him down with too many material concerns, and it was difficult for such a profoundly solitary man to support the closeness of another being – even one as discreet and submissive as Hortense. He did the best he could in part due to his affection for little Paul. In Aix, his mother continued to offer him support and a solid alliance against his father's troubling authority. Unashamed to read his forty-year-old son's mail, the latter discovered his son's erring ways – his marriage and paternity. Nevertheless, Cézanne felt more at home in Aix and L'Estaque than in Paris. He spent every summer at the Jas de Bouffan, and he no longer had to hide Hortense and Paul in Marseille.

One day his day would come, and except in moments of profound discouragement, he realized this. He would receive the recognition that his efforts merited. Though he was never satisfied with the results he obtained, he knew he was on the road to truth, a lonely road, but one which some day people would acknowledge the validity of. At length, he finally did attain the same recognition that had awaited Renoir and Monet. He finally gained entry to the Salon, in 1892, though through a back door, presenting himself as a student of Guillemet; he hung a canvas that has since never been identified, and which at that time went utterly unnoticed. Oh, cruel disappointment!

Cézanne had long aspired to the Salon, and he had finally had his opportunity, but what he failed to understand about this self-imposed goal was that once he had attained it, it no longer meant anything to him. He had entered the Salon through subterfuge, thus avoiding the scrutiny of the jury, but the indifference with which he was met was far worse than the hostility that he usually aroused. From that time, Cézanne (who

was then forty-three years old) entered into a new phase of his life. Bitterly, he withdrew even further inside of himself. His native social hostility increased. And he felt himself growing old: his forty-three years, his baldness, and his weary appearance made him melancholy and he was further saddened by Manet's death. He wrote a will, and became even further ensconced in his southern self-exile, far from the painters of Paris and even farther from the friends of his youth. The only people near to him, his family, failed to understand the importance of his mission. He sought with increasing desperation to uncover the two-fold mystery of nature and painting.

Cézanne turned his back on Paris, his efforts to conquer the city having been in vain. He turned more fervently than ever to this land. It was here that he had put down his roots as a man and gave vent to all his artist's passion; this land possessed him, with its savage light that spurned the softness of the Impressionist brush. But here the demon of the midi raised its head: Cézanne fell in love with Fanny, the maidservant at Jas de Bouffan. It was a scandal in the family. Hortense was unyielding, Fanny was dismissed and Marie (Cézanne's sister) brought order to reign again in the household. Even Zola was involved, somewhat against his will, having been asked by Cézanne to intercept letters which in the end never arrived. The writer was by then famous, and reveled in the glitter of Parisian high society, which he integrated quite skilfully into his work. There was, however, a growing distance between the two old friends – Zola found his friend less and less presentable and more and more bizarre. In his opinion Cézanne was a failure as a painter. He wrote *L'Oeuvre*, the fourth volume in his epic novel *Rougon-Macquart*, the main character of which, Claude Lantier, was directly inspired by Cézanne. The latter, having returned to Aix after a brief escapade, found himself confronted by his domineering sister and his mistress Hortense, who

feared abandonment more than anything else, so much so that every day she waited for him ten kilometres outside of Aix. They even got married! Cézanne had resigned himself to his fate; love affairs were not for him, or rather, the only love affair that was for him was with painting. He bought a donkey and rambled over the countryside; he painted the village of Gardanne and returned to the area around Mont Sainte-Victoire. Sometimes he was accompanied by his old schoolmate Marion, whose friendship he had managed to keep. The younger fellow was a respectable scholar, but his painting had never progressed beyond the amateurish.

Monticelli – an artist whom Cézanne admired, another who had turned his back on Paris, preferring instead Marseille – enjoyed just a fleeting moment of popularity before dying forgotten. Then Cézanne's father – the old patriarch who had already lost his place as head of family to Marie – passed away. Paul junior was fourteen years old when his parents got married, but family life changed little as a result. A good deal more was needed to fill the gap that had grown between them. An occasional trip to Paris gave Cézanne a pause in his life of otherwise steady work and artistic passion. On one of these breaks, the faithful Tanguy introduced him to another fan of Delacroix, an odd Dutch fellow whom Cézanne openly considered quite mad: Vincent van Gogh, who had made a name for himself on the slopes of Montmartre.

It was in this period that Cézanne's passion for Mont Sainte-Victoire became an obsession. And, curiously, though the artist's private life remained highly unstable (but at least with his father's passing he was freed of all material worries), in his painting he achieved that rare harmony he had been seeking for several decades, a balance between intellect and emotion and between design and color. A unique alchemy produced this fruit of Mediterranean bliss.

In this moment the wedding knot was tied between Cézanne and Provence. However, to please Hortense, who was growing bored with provincial life, the family moved back to Paris. They took a home on the Ile Saint-Louis and Cézanne set up his studio on the Left Bank. He rediscovered the Louvre, but not his old friends. He was in touch only with the good Chocquet, who contrived to get his *La Maison du Pendu* exhibited at the 1889 Exposition Universelle.

The subterfuge was successful only in part; the painting was hung where it took a shrewd eye to single it out. On another occasion, he was invited to participate in a collective exhibition (which included van Gogh) in Brussels, but there too he was received with indifference.

Weakened by his diabetes, this series of delusions did not help either Cézanne's state of mind or his health. His mood swings intensified. During one of his rare sightseeing tours, he came across an anti-clerical demonstration that so disturbed him that he disappeared for four days, leaving his wife and child to fend for themselves. This happened during a five-month-long visit in Switzerland, in the course of which it appears that Cézanne suffered greatly. Hortense's whims tried him severely and he was little at peace with his painting. It ended with the couple's separation; one returned to the Jas de Bouffan, and the other passed through Paris before settling in Aix.

Cézanne's return to the land of his self-identity marked a new stage in his artistic and intellectual development. He spent long hours admiring Louis le Nain's *Cardplayers* in the town museum. He rose to the challenge he felt from this painting and did a series on this theme. This was how he usually worked, seeking, as he said, to "realize", to give the best image possible of his subject, one which would be definitive. This was what he demanded of himself though he would never be satisfied with the results.

He was not even aware that meanwhile Paris was

taking note of him. *Père* Tanguy had more and more contracts with visitors and artists, such as Signac, Vuillard, Maurice Denis and others. They went to admire works by this unknown artist, who some believed to be dead! Thanks to Emile Bernard, a monography on the artist from Aix came out. The Impressionists had progressed further along their road, but people began to say that Cézanne was not to be overlooked and that a new generation was appearing on the art scene, with him in the lead. When Tanguy died (Victor Chocquet had preceded him by a little), his collection was auctioned off, though neither Cézanne nor Pissarro or Gauguin profited much by it. There was little competition between buyers for the various works. One man bought five of the six Cézannes up for sale though he had to ask credit for their payment. Without realizing it, Ambroise Vollard had taken his first steps as a great art dealer.

Cézanne never stayed long in one place, and despite everything had managed to keep a few faithful friends. He went to see Monet at Giverny and there he met Auguste Rodin and George Clémenceau, who greatly intimidated him. One day he wrote to the critic Gustave Geffroy, asking to do his portrait. The critic was made to do interminable sittings, before the artist, in despair, abandonned the incomplete protrait, feeling himself incapable of achieving his ends. He fled to the Jas de Bouffan and was received by his mother, who offered him her encouragement as always. And as always, he immersed himself in nature to reveal on his canvases the secret of the energies that he knew eddied beneath the apparent immobility of the sunlight.

About this time, a number of factors contributed to an unexpected shift in public opinion about Cézanne's work. On the part of official art, he had not yet earned the respect of the Salon artists or of the Académie des Beaux-Arts circle, nor indeed did he receive anything but their scorn. However, something happened in 1895 that changed the course of events. Caillebotte had bequeathed his impressive collection of contemporary painting – an anthology of Impressionism, including Cézanne's work – to the Luxembourg museum in Paris. Now, it is well-known that museums do not automatically accept bequests; since the generosity of the donors does not necessarily correspond to the quality of the works making up their estates, the risk of being overrun by clutter is clearly present. The bequests must be put to the test of scholarly an intuitive analysis. In this case, the wave of modern art – represented by the Luxembourg museum – threatened to encroach upon the exclusive territory of the official art milieu. The old guard had to limit as far as possible the inexorable progress of the modern. The decision was theirs – in a Solomon-like judgment, they accepted just half of Caillebotte's bequest.

The most surprising thing was that two of the four Cézannes passed the examination. Around the same time, Ambroise Vollard opened a small shop. Encouraged by this new interest in Cézanne, bolstered by Monet, Renoir and Degas' favorable comments he decided to organize an exhibition of the artist's works. But who was this artist and how could he be contacted? Unbelievable but true, it took a small-scale police investigation to locate him, and with young Paul's help, Vollard communicated his proposal to Cézanne in Aix.

Thus, Vollard, though sorely lacking in funds, organized the 56-year-old painter's first solo exhibition. As for the painter himself, he did not even bother to leave his beloved countryside to attend, though all of his old Impressionist friends were there, as well as a few of the younger generation, who perceived it to be a manifesto of young painting. And a revelation it was! While some of the reviews had not lost the venom of the early days of Impressionism, public taste had evolved somewhat. Other reviews praised the painter, stressing his importance. Above all, the paintings sold, and collectors flocked in all haste to see the exhibition.

Apple Trees.
Merion (Pa.), Barnes Foundation.

Orchard at Pontoise. 1877.
Private collection.

Self-Portrait. 1875.
Private collection.

Near the Pond at the Jas de Bouffan.
Drawing. 1883.

56

Grandes Baigneuses. 1898-1905.
Philadelphia, Philadelphia Museum of Art.

Trois Baigneuses. 1879-82.
Paris, Petit Palais.

Baigneuses sous un Pont. Watercolor. 1895.
New York, Museum of Modern Art.

Les Baigneurs. 1894.
Paris, Louvre.

Self Portrait. Watercolor. 1894.
Private collection.

His success at the exhibition in Aix was not as resounding, although he had participated on the invitation of the Amis des Arts. In truth, he still stirred up scandal in his own province, apart from two or three young admirers. A very gifted young writer, Joachim Gasquet sang his praise and the admiration he lavished on the aging painter seemed to give the latter new courage in yet another moment of crushing doubts and dissatisfaction.

Zola, passing through the Midi, did not even bother to look up his old cohort, though the artist had been his main inspiration for the character Claude Lantier in his novels – a portrayal that contributed instead to the legend of Cézanne as a failed painter.

Vollard, better informed, made the trip to Aix to buy all the Cézannes he could lay his hands on; he was surprised to discover the little esteem that the painter enjoyed among his countrymen. With the excuse that Cézanne's paintings were not worth a sou, they tried to foist the work of local painters on him. However, the dealer did not return to Paris empty-handed. He made some excellent buys, which made it possible for him to represent Cézanne in the capital city and to champion the painter's work. He believed in Cézanne and was counting on him to make some money. (The dealer was anything but a philanthropist.)

In the spring of 1897, the Caillebotte Bequest room at the Luxemboug museum was inaugurated, and Cézanne went to Paris to see his two canvases hung on the museum wall, noting with pride that they had been framed. Imagine, after the Salon had so unyieldingly rejected him! It did not matter that eighteen painters, members of the Institut, complained loudly to the minister about this scandal; he, Cézanne, had made his entry into the museum.

His mother's unexpected death brought him quickly back to Aix. Some months later, Emperaire passed away at the age of sixty-six, marking the end of a life that Cézanne knew had been even more troubled than his own.

Cézanne turned to his 26-years-old son for the affection and comfort he needed. Endowed with an astute practical sense, Paul junior acted as intermediary for Vollard, advising his father to paint more female nudes – they were what sold best. The artist again started to haunt the Louvre, stopping transfixed before works by Poussin and Delacroix, ignoring, however, Fra Angelico's work. He loved the figures, the flesh, solid forms. As his quotations on the art market rose, he decided to do a portrait of Vollard: one hundred and fifteen sittings later – more than four months' work – he abandoned the painting, unable to achieve the results he sought. When Chocquet died, his collection was put up for auction and the best dealers and collectors bid heavily for Cézanne's work.

Never able to stay in Paris for too long, Cézanne returned to Aix. His sister Marie had sold the Jas de Bouffan. He found a place in town, and hired a housekeeper to relieve him of domestic affairs, which he had trouble coping with. He often went to paint near the Château Noir, a property that he would have dearly liked to make his own, going by carriage with a coachman who waited for him each day. Paradoxically, the higher his star rose in the Parisian skies, the more the people of Aix mocked him, perhaps simply out of envy. In 1900, Cézanne was one of the painters selected for the Centennial of French art, sponsored by the Exposition Universelle. This exhibition marked the real triumph of the Impressionists, who finally achieved official glory.

Another "Homage to Cézanne," this time by Maurice Denis: a large canvas, it depicts some of the painters of the younger generation, gathered round a still life by the old master of Aix. André Gide was its purchaser. A few made the pilgrimmage to Aix to see him, as if consulting an elder for his secrets to painting. This was just what the hypochondriac recluse feared most, and he was capable of reactions ranging from the warmest commotion (to the point of tears) to the most choleric outbursts. In any case, it raised his spirits and he made decisions of a practical nature that had been troubling him for some time; he built a small studio on some land that he bought on the road to Lauves. This change, however, did not alter his preference for exteriors and for planting his easel firmly before his subjects.

His wife and son also visited him occasionally, but mainly and to an increasing degree he lived in solitude, under the very authoritarian eyes of his sister Marie, a prickly spinster who kept watch over him as if over a child, and had the housekeeper count out his pocket money. As for this housekeeper, according to Perruchot, once when Cézanne was away she burnt his sketches of the Baigneuses because they were nude!

Emile Bernard fresh off the boat after eleven years in Egypt, took the opportunity to pay a visit on Cézanne. Bernard was, after all, the author of the first important book on the painter. The two men had never met before, and Bernard remained in Aix for a full month with his wife and children, working at the ground floor of the Lauves studio. He closely observed Cézanne as he painted the *Grandes Baigneuses*. The artist worked on this painting for almost ten years, without ever finding – as he himself stated – the center around which it was to be constructed.

The Salon d'automne of 1904 dedicated an entire room to him. Thirty of his works were shown and once again he found himself at the center of a heated debate. The younger generation of artists embraced him as one of their own, as the one who was paving the way for them. The influential review *Mercure de France* published a broad survery of contemporary art in which one of the questions directly concerned Cézanne. The answers provided by the artists and intellectuals consulted cannot be said to have revealed great insight, as irony and insult still prevailed. The artist, consumed by his diabetes, felt death closing in on him, though he was so far from his goal. Sure of his greatness as a painter, and aware of the quality of the example he was setting and of the works that he would be leaving behind, he was far from achieving what he had sought all his life in painting – this remains a mystery, a truth that is yet to be revealed. But nothing could stop him from working. He had sworn to himself to die with his painthbrush in hand, because he had given his life to painting, and it had no meaning except through painting. The summer of 1906 was a torrid one, and Cézanne painted by the seaside though it was exhausting. That autumn, the weather was pleasant, but the coachman asked for a raise in pay, and Cézanne decided to do without his services. On October 15, he was painting in a clearing near the Lauves when a sudden cloudburst took him by surprise. He continued unperturbed by the storm, leaving only when he was ready. Loaded down with his artist's materials, he fainted. Somebody found him and helped him back home. The following day, against the doctor's orders, he set out again, as usual. It was his last outing, and his final days were spent delirious in bed. On October 22, 1906, Paul Cézanne died. One year later, the Salon d'automne honored him with a retropective showing fifty-seven paintings. At the same time, the French government turned down the gift offered by the new owner of the Jas de Bouffan: the paintings that Cézanne had left behind. Less than twenty years later, his town named an avenue after him, and from then on Glory – alas posthumous – accompanied his name.

Contemporary art criticism correctly teaches us to see how a work is painted rather to look at what it depicts. Considering how differently two painters can treat the same subject, it is logical to conclude that the subject of a painting is of secondary importance. However, the painting is an

Renoir. *Portrait of Cézanne.* 1880.
Private collection

Portrait of Cézanne. 1879-82.
Berne, Kunstmuseum.

image of something, after all; what the painter has chosen to paint should not be taken lightly, even if sometimes it seems more a question of chance or expedience than choice. Modern psychology teaches us that no choice is random. We shall not overlook, then, the subjects of Cézanne's painting. They can be classified into five categories, according to traditional criteria: self-portraits, portraits, still lifes, scenes and landscapes.

An artist's search to penetrate the secrets of his own face is always deeply suggestive. It is an encounter with himself, an enquiry into his own identity. He asks, "Who am I?" – a question that no one can answer, one that underlies the restless search for truth that characterizes every artist's life. Cézanne left us twenty or so self-portraits showing various facets of himself between the ages of 20 and 60 years. His first portrait reveals a young man with an intense gaze, a black mustache crossing his face, a brooding and somewhat mistrusting look, the head tilted slightly forward, as if to show his determined brow. Forty years later, the same man appears in three-quarters profile, wearing a beret of the sort with a drooping brim; his mustache is longer and by then gone grey, like the pointed beard he has grown. His eyebrows are arched as he gazes sadly at the viewer. This painting presents a melancholy man; he looks older than his sixty years, wasted by his diabetes and his lifelong struggle to live and to paint, that is to be fully himself in a milieu that could not give him the space he needed to blossom, but from which he could not – and not just for economic reasons – detach himself. The catalogues list two names for this painting: *Cézanne with Pointed Beard* an *Portrait of the Artist with Beret*. This is only portrait he left of himself with this style of beard, which lengthened his face; usually he had a full beard which made it seem more round.

It is the only one in which he is capped by a beret, and among the few in which he wears a hat;

most often he depicted himself bare-headed. It is possible that his baldness had advanced to a stage that he could not bear the sight of it – but it is more likely that Cézanne used the dark mass of the beret to create an artistic effect. Its soft form and lack of luminosity – as opposed to the more distinct structure of a hat or cap – were enough to interest him. It is difficult to identify in this sad old man the determined and tough young man of Cézanne's first self-portrait. The weight of a lifetime separates them and all the energy of the first went toward the somewhat obdurate wisdom of the second. ("No painter, said John Rewald, has ever gone as far as Cézanne in stripping away all complacency and self-indulgence, to offer this reflection of himself.") Of course, the subject had changed, but so had the painter's way of seeing himself. We can interpret the painted subject's gaze as that of the artist in the moment in which he painted it: there, piercing, searching, analytic; and here, deep, empty, indifferent, jaded, synthetic. All this is reflected in the eyes and the vitality of the gaze; Impressionism, indeed, quickly became the study of the art of perception, an apology for the optical sensation. But the eyes of the painter as a young man smitten by Courbet and Delacroix – they hold such romantic fervor! It is as if Cézanne were saying to us, "The eyes aren't as important as they seem; for a painter, the eyes are not everything."

There is, of course, the opposite interpretation, that the eyes are so important, so essential that it is impossible to depict them; they become taboo. We shall never know. But the fact remains that the subjects eyes are rarely defined in Cézanne's portraits, as if he could not bring himself to paint them, as if he feared them, as if he could not bear the gaze of his subjects (the sittings with Cézanne went on for so long that the subjects may well have gotten a lackluster look), not to mention that of the painting.

Cézanne could not bear any physical contact

(an uninvited touch of the hand caused him to fly into a rage) – could it be that a person's gaze had the same burning effect? A look at the range of portraits he painted shows that he rarely met his subjects' eyes, that he minimized the eye, emptying it of its sight so that it blended into the contours of the face, or at least attenuating it to the extent possible. A number of his self-portraits – including the ones mentioned above – suggest that the only gaze that he could bear to meet was his own.

For the painter, to paint an eye that emits a gaze, along with the facial contours that contain it is no small problem – especially for a painter who draws with his brush, modeling the forms with color (the eye is a concave shape while the apple is convex, but curiously no critic has ever proposed this obverse of the much-discussed fruit as the true forbidden fruit). The closer the subject is to the foreground, the more pressing the problem becomes; the best way to avoid the eye is to push the subject into the background, as Cézanne did in the three portraits of Vallier, where the light filtering through the foliage justifies the absence of relief and detail. (A different example can be seen in the Tate Gallery's V 715, where the gardener's hat falls squarely over his eyes.)

It is said that Cézanne never took a personal interest in the subjects he painted and that only the play of light on the shapes and the textures mattered to him; he probably selected his models from those closest to him because they were the most easily available. However, this judgment seems hasty, since, as we know, Cézanne was not indifferent by nature. It also makes us wonder how he managed to keep aloof of his subject's personalities in the course of the endless sittings that he required. Did he reduce them to objects without humanity? And, should he have struggled against failure so many times, when an apple would have done just as well? The rapport between an artist and his models throughout the history of painting would be well worth studying in detail, and coincidentally it was one of Cézanne's greatest disciples who devoted a significant portion of his life's work to this question (though in terms of painting): Pablo Picasso.

The painter exercises a power over his subject, whether the latter is a paid professional or has voluntarily offered himself, passive and immobile, to the painter. Cézanne very frequently painted his wife and it is understandable that she yielded more or less agreeably to the will of her difficult husband. But why he did not paint his mother, sister and son more often remains an open question. Also interesting is that he tried to paint all the men, his friends, who most counted in his life: Emile Zola, Joachim Gasquet, Gustave Geffroy, Victor Chocquet. Part of this gift of painting, then, was to consolidate the links of a relationship, to crystallize them into an image in which the painter defined his perception of the other.

These vague remarks cannot satisfy our curiosity and serve merely to ask a question that until now has been overlooked. Indeed, our curiosity is further roused by the fact that several strangers from the area agreed to pose for him, though we do not know under what conditions.

Cézanne's work shows his great fascination for the human figure. The importance of this has been played down in favor of his still lifes and landscapes, but it would be well worth further study. With a man as solitary, almost misanthropic, as Cézanne, the importance he attributed to human presence in his works strikes us as a way to compensate for his existential problems, especially in interpersonal relationships. It is unfair to say that Cézanne reduced his subjects to the status of mannequins, as his images are far from inexpressive and he captures the essence of the individuals he portrayed. No less than in his self-portraits, he penetrated beyond the formal wrappings and managed to reveal the subject's inner life, even though the eyes played a very minor role in this.

Portrait of Vallier.
Private collection.

Toulouse-Lautrec. *Portrait of Emile Bernard.* 1886.
Private collection.

The Sailor.
Washington, National Gallery of Art.

Standing Peasant.
Merion (Pa.), Barnes Foundation.

Boy Bent over a Book. Drawiing. 1885.

Pissarro. *Portrait of Cézanne.* 1874.
Private collection.

Moreover, only the eyes were obscured in Cézanne's work; the gaze persisted. Its direction can be intuited, but it is never stressed and it is never probing. In this absent gaze that only rarely pentrates beyond the canvas, I see an expression of Cézanne's fear of the other's scrutiny, his fear of others. It is as if he feared being touched by a gaze, similar to his intolerance of physical contact with others.

A gaze for Cézanne was a gesture that he mistrusted, and in his painting he tended to repress it by softening and shading it. Whether the subject was shown in partial – if not full – profile or frontally, his painting style excluded precision in draftsmanship and the resulting image was unclear. This explains the many blackened gazes and the empty eye sockets culminating in the skulls where the eyes were no more than cavities (and yet this absence-of-eyes seems to stare fixedly at us).

Biographers agree that Cézanne's relationship with his mother was one of complicity. His father, on the other hand, was strongly authoritarian, and commanded awe and respect. It is strange, then, that he never did a portrait of his mother. It may be that he felt that she was too close to him to be able to see her, to rest his critical painter's gaze on her. On perhaps there is some deeper reason why he never conserved her image, in this way somehow punishing her, expunging her. Or perhaps again, he wished to keep for himself an everpresent image he had of her, refusing to crystallize it or to communicate it to anybody.

What taboos surrounded the subject of his mother? The father, though he had never encouraged Cézanne to paint had the honor of being painted three times – one time more than Marie, the elder of his two sisters and the one who inherited the father's authority in the family. The last-born Rose remained in the shadows, like her mother.

The three portraits of Louis-Auguste Cézanne have in common a single peculiarity: not only does the subject's gaze escape us, but it is clear that he feels only disdain his painter-son, and that he never cared much for him. That his son was painting a handsome portrait of him did not interest him in the least; he was resolutely absorbed in reading his newspaper. He permitted his son to paint him, but made it clear that he was not going to be a participant in this process. His son played this same game of indifference by painting it, underlining the distance that separated him from his father by representing him in full height (wide angle). This was a pose he rarely adopted, and it recurred only much later in his career (portrait of Chocquet, of an Aix local, of the gardener Vallier). Marie was shown in a more conventional manner, in the two close-up portraits, but in the first of these her eyes are kept downcast. The gaze is essential to the portrait.

While the 20th century witnessed the diffusion of a new concept of the landscape tending towards more natural images (it became a leading component of decor), the still life maintained its traditional role as a painterly exercise, even if it too evolved conceptually. From the masterpiece of precision, with *trompe-l'oeil* effects where the artist's materials and technique had to be invisible, it became a pretext for other forms of mastery, lending itself to all the manipulation that the artist wished to operate on it. The still life played a fundamental role in the history of European art, where the role of the subject was of diminishing importance. A history of the themes in still life – such as the military, pastoral, symbolic – would be well worth writing; the choice of the subject is always meaningful, and both sociology and psychology could contribute useful insights to the relationship between the painter and the objects he depicts in his paintings.

At the beginning, Cézanne adopted the conventions inherited from the century before which had been developed in particular by Chardin. The composition was made up of domestic objects set on a table: plates, glasses, tableware, pots, bottles, fruits and vegetables (the lasting and the ephemeral, the opaque and the transparent...) supplied a vast array of shapes textures and colors for the artist to manipulate at his pleasure. Cézanne tried them all at the outset, but it is well-known that one type of fruit took the lead...

Another traditional theme, the bouquet of flowers (dahlias, geraniums, petunias, etc.), appears throughout Cézanne's oeuvre. Through it, he perfected his use of color and it forced him to adopt a style profuse with brushstrokes and tones. Is was also a way to paint from life in the studio – and this was not to be overlooked by a painter as enamoured of nature's minute changes as Cézanne. Flowers and fruit presented only one drawback: though they offered the advantage of being motionlessness, they altered day by day, changing color and finally fading or rotting. And though Cézanne from the start was capable of painting a picture very quickly, he was a very slow painter by habit – and increasingly so. To capture life, which he felt was his duty as a painter, became impossible for him, for it cannot be confined to the fixity of the painting. Every painter in his own way must confront the question of time; Impressionism had offered a unique solution by seeking to faithfully record the instant. Cézanne was, to the contrary, concerned with the essence of things, quite in keeping with his traditionalist, religious outlook.

Cézanne's thematic choices became increasingly simple and ordinary. The only religious subject to which he felt deeply drawn was contemplative. (Neither biography nor mythology have a place in Cézanne's work; in spite of the influence the painter attributed to Delacroix among his precursors, he himself was far from being a painter of history.) The skull appeared in his work from about 1865, in some unoriginal compositions – an image of death whose gaze though blank fixates the painter. The book and candlestick suggest that reading and meditation should teach us the vanity of all things. And if painting too were the vain, absurd, useless issue of a blameworthy ambition? Cézanne was a deep-thinking man, haunted by religious and metaphysical convictions that conditioned his life and underlay all of his work. Twenty-five years after this painting, he painted one in which the skulls multiplied, mounting up and falling into ranks like in the catacombs or like the apples in his still lifes. In a lifework dominated by a delicate sensuality and an harmonious and insatiable conception of nature (not without a slight sense of melancholy), these skulls are a clamorous intrusion. They seem to be the resurgence of something that Cézanne had always kept hidden, even from himself: a private tragedy, the unexpected signs of which no longer had anything in common with conventional themes. At 60 years of age, Cézanne, who suffered more from attacks of morbidity than his painting would lead one to believe, was haunted by death. Consumed by his diabetes, he felt prematurely aged. He had known little joy in his life – he had been an aesthete and mystic in search of deep truths and bent on an impossible task. Painting was a stressing experience for him, one that left him with a sense of failure, a persistent feeling of unfulfilment. It is hard for us to imagine when standing before one of his delightful images that its apparent lightness was the fruit of a dramatic struggle, that it was the precipitate of a lengthy process of alchemy in which he had failed, however, to transform his character made up of violent contrasts between romantic fervor and a classical obsession with structure.

The apple as recurrent motif in Cézanne's works is intructive here. Meyer Shapiro studied its symbolic implications, calling into play the artist's friendship with Zola (the outset of which was signalled by the gift of a basket of this fruit) and Cézanne's sensual obsession, though his

Still Life.
Oslo, National Gallery of Art.

Blue Vase. 1885-87.
Paris, Louvre.

Flowers in Little Delft Vase. 1873-75.
Paris, Louvre.

Still Life on Bureau.
Cambridge (Mass.), Fogg Art Museum.
M. Wertheim Collection.

Green Apples. 1873.
Paris, Louvre.

Still Life with Apples. Watercolor.
Vienna, Kunsthistorische Museum.

Still Life with Apples and Oranges.
Paris, Louvre.

Still Life with Plate of Apples. 1873-77.
Private collection.

Still Life with Black Clock.
Private collection.

Still Life with Skull and Candlestick.
Private collection.

87

actual experience of women cannot have rivalled that of his fantasies. Hortense, it seems, rather quickly became a long-distance companion and in his mythology the apple represented the woman, the feminine element in all its roundness, which otherwise appears only in the large compositions of *Les Baigneuses* – those great paintings that revolutionized art, heralding the work of Picasso, but which, it must be said, are at times clumsy in their praise of women.

A man of the French Midi, who spent most of his childhood and maturity roaming the countryside, painting (though we note in passing that he rarely painted fruit trees), Cézanne showed an insatiable fascination for this fruit: the apple with its enticing roundness (could it also be the depiction of the mother's breast, the mother whom he always avoided painting?) And colors! Reds and yellows full of light.

Curiously, the even more feminine peach did not attract the painter. Only one youthful painting shows this fruit, and it is in imitation of a painting at the Aix museum. However, there are at least two reasons for this: the peach has a greater absorption of light and, above all, it is more perishable than the apple – it has a lower resistance to the passing of time.

Cézanne never denied wishing to conquer Paris with an apple, following the mythological example of Paris who in his judgment of the three Goddesses offered the fruit to Venus. Indeed, he seemed to be saying, "What matters is not the apple but the painting that makes the painter". But in Cézanne's case the apple was clearly not just an object like any other.

Cézanne was little more than 20 years old when he painted *The Judgment of Paris*, a somewhat clumsy attempt, where the three female nudes seem rather embarrassed to be parading their nudity about the countryside. Paris remains clothed, his hand resting on his chosen "fairest", though his other hand still grasps the golden apple, which he holds out in a final moment of indecision to one of the two other beauties who are leaving, piqued about not having been chosen. The painter used the apple here in a clever compositional trick, making it the keystone of the painting. It does not yet possess the symbolic value of the sensuous apples in his mature work, and what Paris is offering to the goddesses is certainly not the maternal breast... The importance of this painting instead lies in the fact that it was the first composition of nudes and landscape painted by Paul Cézanne, a first version of what culminated in the *Grandes Baigneuses*, although here, the female figures stand out against a conventional backdrop. Cézanne had previously demonstrated greater painting skill, even more talent in his copies of masterpieces. Thus some mechanism had already been sparked whereby he was not painting as "well" as he was able.

Stiff movements; thick, unwieldy figures: could this poor treatment of the triple female image reflect the young man's insecurities on account of his inexperience? This theory is not absurd but it is insufficient: if Cézanne did not draw very well here, it was because he had already ceased to draw – that is, he drew with his paintbrush directly from the palette. He could have continued Ingres' course on the path of "graceful charm" but instead chose another challenge, following the example of Courbet and Delacroix. The figure is not simply the play of lines that makes up this superficial wrapping of skin; there is the weight of the flesh and bones, a solid and constructed feeling. The figure of the *Bather at the Rock* is a good example of this concern for the material, the static vision of the body that Cézanne developed in his female bathers as he was studying the modeling to solve the difficult problems of integrating the form-figure in the background-landscape without indulging in the luxury of haze, without relying on the force of the structures.

The matrons in *The Temptation of Saint*

Anthony show a striking carnal opulence and how Cézanne's attention to the composition already started to distort the figures, making them rigid: the neck of the central figure is plainly contorted. At 30 years of age, Cézanne was seeking his way in a web of influences that linked Delacroix, Courbet, Daumier and Manet... To these influences, Cézanne added his own brand of romantic realism which allowed him to express the violence of his personality, rather than the passions that fueled it during these early years of his painting career.

The Flaubertian theme of St. Anthony had less to do with an aesthete's resistance to temptation than with the invasion of a solitary man's spirit by a host of his own phantasms. It is about desire, a desire without an object, condemned to the imaginary. But the saint in this painting is a secondary figure in the background who appears to be struggling against a woman who is approaching him. (In truth, there is nothing to indicate that it is a woman, just the shape of a backside – and the figure is quite ambiguous.) The true subject of the painting is the group of three women that the painter attempted to evidence, three women like the three goddesses but painted in a more life-like way and with more self-confidence. In Cézanne there is the Christian who does not want to see and the painter who wants to see everything – a conflict which seems to have been resolved in his two versions of *A Modern Olympia*, where the male figure (no doubt the painter) has moved into the foreground and is not ashamed to let his gaze rest upon the woman curled up on the bed. This theme culminates in the two versions of *Après midi à Naples*, especially in the second where the male figure, nude, has joined the female on the bed, in an attitude of relaxation and self-satisfaction. The rendering of the figures has been simplified, resulting in the solid unity scarce on detail that characterizes Cézanne's work. In this painting, Cézanne has surpassed Delacroix' synthetic mastery – as a look at the latter's contemporary *Apotheosis* reveals. It is one of his first great achievements in terms of the flattened perspective, a break from the great tradition of the Renaissance. It recalls Baudelaire (the painter was a faithful reader of the poet), and his dream of a paradise where there is "only luxury, calm and delight." From here on in, this hedonism little by little overtook Cézanne's romantic fervor, and rather than movement he tended to depict a motionless harmony where movement seems to be suspended, fixed in space for eternity but animated by a vibration that unites the elements of the painting, charging them with a vital tension that flows between them.

We have come to the period in which Cézanne painted his Bathers – one of the three main themes identified by the critics, together with the apples and Mont Sainte-Victoire. The bathers frequently appear in threesomes, as in the Barnes Foundation painting, where for the first time the painter used the scenic device for which the painting became famous: the limbs of the trees orching over to frame the scene, preventing the landscape and the perspective from opening up onto the sky. Cézanne pursued this theme throughout the 1880s in a series of paintings where he sought to augment their complexity by changing the number and positions of the figures, culminating in the *Cinque Baigneuses* at the Basel Kunstmuseum.

I am not sure that Cézanne achieved more in his successive canvases, especially in the three versions of the *Grandes Baigneuses* which are generally acclaimed as the peak of his career. In them he clearly triumphed in the decorative intensity and the blend of colors infusing the scene with a light that leaves little room for shade, but the composition loses its force, and the figures their three-dimensionality. Here, the pictorial quality, which is the fruit of Cézanne's personal alchemy, has evolved at the cost of a physical sensation, of a sensual presence. The sense of desire is no longer transmitted, and it is as if Cézanne – who had always felt embarrassment at painting nudes from life – had achieved this highly moral victory of no longer seeing the body, instead selecting and applying the parts as if they were part of a pictorial lexicon. Such sublimation also left its mark on his hunger to get to the bottom of his painter's passion, to achieve artistic satisfaction, even if momentary – especially in light of the fact that it was accompanied by his frequent inability now to complete a canvas. But also, Cézanne changed the quality of his oil painting, thinning it down to the point that it almost seemed a watercolor, giving it a transparency that attenuated the figures and dissolved nature, though he attempted to use the trees to resurrect the structure of a Gothic nave.

Cézanne was launched on a trajectory that could only lead to the annulment of the human figure. It was impossible for him to come to terms with it; though he had known how to paint it almost too early on, he had prohibited himself to see it. The apotheosis of the *Grandes Baigneuses* rejects the bodies that Manet had so daringly introduced to the landscape, at the threshold between Romanticism and Impressionism. The last time Cézanne painted the human figure (in a return to the motif, but where the motif is inert) was in his *Plaster Love*, the very title of which seems to confirm the annulment which reduced Baudelaire's sensual revery to a prosaic image teetering on the edge of mockery. Another parting attempt at the human figure was that of the gardener Vallier, who seems just about to dissolve into the trees. To make the body disappear, to thus challenge the original sin which had always persecuted him – this seems to have been Cézanne's great temptation. And he succeeded, since it was with the landscape that he best developed his painting style.

Cézanne's landscapes are above all Romantic.

He was most influenced by Courbet and a host of painters of Provence whom he had admired at the Aix museum, and of whom his friend Monticelli was the privileged heir. The chromatic and tonal contrasts highlight the rigorous compositions. Under Pissarro's influence, dating to his stay in Anvers-sur-Oise (1872), Cézanne became acquainted with Impressionism and its emphasis on the subjective vision and the individual sensibility. Thereafter, his drawing lost its linear precision, and he achieved depth through the use of color. This was Cézanne's greatest contribution to the art of painting. Let us recall that Impressionism was born in the area of Ile de France, and the special light of this region – which later attracted painters from the world over to Paris – was determinant in the dawning and development of this movement. The Seine and Oise valleys offered to the avant-garde painters of the late 19th century more than just subjects to paint; there, a spirit of moderation reigned, one suited to the development of sensibilities susceptible to a particular perception of reality that demanded their attention. It offered them an alternative to the epic excesses of Romanticism, continuing on the path of the Barbizon painters who had already contributed much to the emergence of a modern perception of nature already somewhat melancholy in the face of expanding industrialization. The dialectic that underlies the urban and rural themes of Impressionism played no small part in this. Cézanne had made the trip from Aix, but it was an exile from even further away – Pissarro – who introduced him to the landscape of the Ile de France and coached him on the Impressionist use of color, limiting the importance of the line and of shadow.

There was no clean break, as this was not in Cézanne's character. His pace was one of slow evolution accompanied by deep reflection, cautious progress not without some backtracking for the sake of verification. Venturi correctly noted that Cézanne was at Anvers-sur-Oise during his stay with Dr. Gachet, when his painting began to show the density of air and the vibration of light that dissolves forms, distorts volumes and clouds the clarity of vision and depth typical of theoretical – and not actually experienced – perspective. This two-fold reliance on optical laws and personal sensibilities gave rise to Impressionism and it is what won Cézanne over to the movement. Instinctively, he already tended towards this two-fold focus, and he also found in the Parisian movement a like-mindedness that drew him out of his provincial solitude.

La Maison du Pendu confirms that this was a turning-point in Cézanne's life and his work. The painting is a seminal work, a milestone marking one of the artist's rare moments of satisfaction. His signature, which appears rather rarely on his canvases, is proof of this achievement, and Cézanne agreed several times to exhibit it. Victor Chocquet was not mistaken when he acquired the painting through a trade with another collector. The composition is solidly constructed around two imposing masses of houses. One, surely that of the hanged man, is shown frontally; the other is seen from its rear and barely more than the softly suspended thatched roof can be made out.

The right-hand side of the painting is dominated by greenish tones, practically without any design (simply a patch of sky above this roof which eclipses the horizon line). Its extreme simplicity contrasts with the complexity of the left-hand side, where there is a rock in the foreground and then a road that opens up in the middle of the painting, running obliquely across it. There there is a triangle-shaped grassy embankment, with a double vertical line formed by the two trees framing the painting, upon which the viewer's gaze rests. Behind them, and cut in two by them, is the house. One of the two parts is lighter and shows the three black rectangles of the windows and the door, and a triangular portico which echos the roof of the first house. Behind it, rise two trees to the height of the canvas in the distance. Between the houses, the crowded roofs of the town can be seen and above them the landscape in the distance, with slightly rolling hills and a whitish sky near the horizon, turning blue in a horizontal band just at the top of the canvas. In this surprising painting, the eye is not simply invited to follow one or another of these three axes; the richness of this composition is owing to the interpenetration of its various planes so that the landscape is no longer divided into these three main sections. The eye shifts constantly from one to the other: rocks, thatched roof, trees, the hanged man's house, village, horizon. And this is made possible only by the subtle play of light linking the volumes to one another and by the consistency of the air which extends in a unitary mass from the foreground into the distance. The perspective is not created with a vanishing point but it opens out onto a plane at which the gaze stops and which keeps the horizon near to the viewer. This bond between objects, shapes and background, between mass and space, is what Cézanne is all about.

In *La Maison du Pendu*, Cézanne realized his inner vision for the first time. He was then 33 years old and neither with still lifes nor with portraits had he yet been able to express so clearly his pictorial aims. It must be understood – and it is here where we see what distinguished him from the Impressionists – that he could not have done it without a strong foundation in draftsmanship and in composition or had he ceded to the dematerializatoin of objects which was often a weakpoint of Impressionism until Monet developed it in his Waterlilies. In this key canvas, Cézanne, in utter contrast to the classical tradition exemplified by Ingres, appears as a skilful draftsman who has not yet learned how to integrate design and painting. The painting does not cancel the design, but it replaces the line with the brushstroke, which in itself is not very compli-

Mont Sainte-Victoire.
Basel, Kunsthaus.

cated: Impressionism, in restricting itself to the surface of things and the first visual impression, had easily solved this problem.

Cézanne went further since he managed to conserve the consistency of things, the substance of volume. He was fascinated by light, and discovered in the Ile de France that air too has its own density. Earthbound, he did not lose himself in the air nor in the sea, he was a Southerner who learned to see in his homeland how the light strikes hard against things and carves them into space. And it seems that unlike Picasso, Cézanne was able to swallow in one gulp all that Impressionism had to teach him about light (even though the movement itself was still groping for its way) and go one step further by integrating it into his search for a broader synthesis, where the light was no longer the dominant element at the cost of others.

It is in his landscapes that his divergence from the Impressionists can be seen most clearly (since Impressionism is based primarily on the landscape), and by taking nature as his guide, he developed his two-fold law of simultaneous contrast and the dematerialization of lines and volumes in the light. In the years that followed Cézanne's disassociation from the Impressionist group, in part provoked by the failed exhibition of 1877, he focused on form, paying great attention to composition, while his friends, especially Monet, went in the opposite direction. In his famous *Small Bridge* of 1879, one of his richest canvases, Cézanne very skilfully complimented the curve of the arch with a complex play of straight horizontal and vertical lines that appear on successive planes. Elsewhere, the course of a road was enough to render the composition unique.

Or just the bend in a tree trunk.

Trees... In this period around 1885, Cézanne gave them a special role, letting them overrun his canvases until they obstructed the conventional view which, extending into the distance, is con-structed on the horizon line and forces the artist to paint the sky. He returned to the trees that he had climbed as a boy, at the Jas de Bouffan and at Bibémus, and he gazed at them as a painter, leafy or bare, dramatic in their sinuous lines and their way of bulking large against the background, sometimes even concealing it.

He then concentrated on his draftsmanship, defining each element of the painting and concentrating more on composition than on dissolution to achieve unity: tree trunks and branches make up a repetitive structure that emerges almost on a single plane. He continued to paint his views of villages seen in close-up or from afar, his seascapes at l'Estaque with their solidly constructed planes, and finally, Mont Sainte-Victoire, the mountain that became a myth, the modest hill that Cézanne made his greatest accomplishment as a landscape painter whether in the highly diluted, more intimate watercolors or the heavily "troweled" oils: the recurrence of Mont Sainte-Victoire in Cézanne's work suggests that it was a dominant point of reference to which he could not refrain from returning. In his final, obsessive series of canvases Cézanne pushed his studies to an extreme, achieving maximum simplicity. This mountain, and there is no coincidence that it is today along with the apple, symbolic of him. It was with these two themes that the painter seems to have made his greatest breakthroughs; he dedicated his best efforts to them and it would not be correct to imagine that this choice of theme is arbitrary. One may well say that Cézanne was Cézanne whatever he painted, but we feel that his dual obsession is an intriguing mystery, the solution to which lies in long-forgotten clues of his past. While at times we may sense even in the most ordinary subjects Cézanne's subconscious rising to the surface, we are in no position to analyze its mechanisms or to unveil its artifices. However, we may explore the plastic role the mountain played in his painting at the close of his career as a painter; it is a massive shape, clearly defined within the space it occupies between the earth and the sky, easing the transition between the opaque solid and the transparent fluid. It has a simple shape, like the apple, the volume and substance of which it was necessary to render, the density of which had to be expressed, all the while maintaining the awareness of its being only one element of the landscape: extending before it was the land, the plain, little by little rising into its slopes, leading up to the mountain. It was as if the mountain had roots that drove deep down into the earth, extending far into the plain, moving in closer to us, at the base of the painting. It is as if the mountain were the result of the land's mighty effort to raise itself up, showing all the tension of its geological framework. Looking closely, beyond this peaceable image of a landscape, it is impossible not to feel the gradual thrust of the telluric forces. This is what Cézanne evoked from beneath the surface of things, while the Impressionists were satisfied with an image. He was not content – as they were – to look and to let himself be permeated by the image; his gaze was nourished by his impassioned relationship with the world and with the land. This rambler of the countryside would stop and plant his easel in the ground as a torero plunges his banderillas into the bull's shoulder muscles, then he would start a duel in which he would face a fascinating object and advance towards it, armed only with his rich knowledge of it. But the painter, unlike the torero, never came into contact with his subject; the Sainte-Victoire was inaccessible, the painter never scaled his mountain, the image-maker kept aloof from his subject. Cézanne ended his days before this mountain as Oedipus before the Sphinx; in response to the painter's questions, the mountain could only offer its own image, the image it permitted him to take. But the image, like the thing, escaped him. To the inaccessible corresponds the unachieved. While the apple filled the

void left by women and Cézanne succeeded in capturing its essence, Mont Sainte-Victoire offered him a new frontier: how to paint a landscape that resolves into a mass, and how to paint the qualities of a mass that is so far away that it appears to be without density. And what is Mont Sainte-Victoire if not a plane that becomes a mass, or the force of a plane trying to emerge from itself. With a painter whose constant quest was to bring perspective back to a plane, does this not seem to express a fundamental contradiction that confirms what we know about his always sensitive and sometimes explosive nature, driven by a muted fervor that he normally managed to keep under control? It seems that Cézanne always held something back, in his life as in his painting: something like an external force that came into conflict with one that deep inside of him tended to expand. Cézanne's best paintings of the Mont Sainte-Victoire portray this conflict between a centrifugal force and a centripetal one. The sky has a substantiality that weighs on the mountain; its density is equal to that of the earth. This is what helps prevent the top of the painting from vanishing into the ether. This is the lot of the land, condemned by nature to bear the weight of the sky. Cézanne lightened the land and weighed down the sky. He joined them in equal colored harmonies and he treated them on the same plane, defeating the false sense of perspective as well as the illusory transparence.

Moreover, Cézanne's ultimate theme of Mont Sainte-Victoire is exemplary among his works for its expression of a basic dialectic, for its exploration of problems of space. An urgent, personal question was thus transformed into a pictorial question of extreme perspicacity. The painter was engaged in a violent struggle with himself.

"Painting is a funny thing," Cézanne once confided to Jules Borély. But he never ceased to explore this funny thing (to which he had dedicated his life), focusing not so much on the impulse that drove him to paint as on the goals he set out to achieve and the means to do so. He never fully developed his ideas, since he was neither a man of letters nor a theoretician, but there is available, nevertheless, a large body of documents, including his personal correspondence, and a recently published compilation of notices about Cézanne provided by painters, critics and friends which will be useful to us in trying to understand what he thought about painting in general and his own in particular.

The two sources combined may have been useful in attempting a brief summary of his ideas and their development, point by point. However, we felt it preferable to not present on the same level information culled from written correspondence and information derived from conversations reported to have taken place; in the latter case, the human element comes into play. We cannot be certain of the accuracy of reports made by admirers who in most cases did not lack in preconceptions about this eccentric artist of Aix. Therefore, we have deciced to first analyze Cézanne's writing, that is, the surviving letters that have been collected and published, and then to study what he is reported to have said, with varying degrees of credibility.

The volume containing Cézanne's letters is divided into three parts corresponding to the three main stages of his life, that is, in the evolution of his experience and his artistic thought:

1) the letters of his youth through to his discovery of Impressionism (the formative years 1858-1870);

2) the letters during his phase of development, reflecting Cézanne's doubts about Impressionism and the questions that led him to abandon it (1872-1890). Zola played an important role in these first two parts.

3) the letters of his maturity in which he attempts to hone down the theories which step by step, simply but rigorously, he has established.

Here he was writing to people younger than he, who were anxious to grasp his theories and inclined to admire him. The first of Cézanne's letters that John Rewald found for publication in his edition of the artist's collected letters is dated April 9, 1858, and is addressed to Zola. Its writer was then 19 years old, and in it did not yet mention painting.

Rather, it is crammed with clumsy and ironic poetry, typical of the way in which two well-read young people would address each other. Cézanne did not yet speak of painting, but there is one sentence that stands out among the rest of the banalities: "Remember the pine tree here planted at the edge of the arch, pushing its hairy head out over the gully that spread out at its foot?" How many times would he have later painted this same tree? As if in the talk of an adolescent with an alternately sunny or melancholy disposition, a deeper note resonates, heralding a truth to be uncovered in later years... Soon afterwards, painting came into the picture. In a letter addressed once again to Zola, Cézanne copied a long poem, accompanied by a watercolor (now lost), on the theme of "Cicero Fulminating Catalina upon Disovering the Plot of this Citizen of Sullied Honor." In his self-commentary, Cézanne did not appear to take himself very seriously when he boasted "the incomparable beauty contained in this admirable watercolor."

Thus, painting did not yet seem to be a deep-rooted interest, and it certainly took a backseat to poetry, which continued to be the main topic of discussion netween the two young men, even when Cézanne began his law studies, and even if a drawing occasionally graced a letter. Not all of these have been conserved, of course, and we only know of Cézanne's letters to Zola in the period 1860-62 through references the latter made in letters to others or in his replies to Cézanne. A letter from Zola to Cézanne dated March 3, 1860 is the first from which we can learn that the two friends had been dabbling in paint for some time and that Cézanne for two years had been anxiously awaiting the moment in which he could terminate his law studies in favor of the life of an artist. This is the famous letter in which Zola gave Cézanne detailed instructions on what to do upon the latter's arrival in Paris. However, Zola commented "We often write of poetry in our letters, but the words sculpture and painting come up only rarely, if ever."

Cézanne wrote little to his friends about painting, about his vocation and his doubts, doubts which were greater than one might think, judging from the little that is said about them. Cézanne's reserve in his correspondence with his dearest friend is all the same puzzling, both because for some buried, personal reason he avoided expressing this burning question and found it difficult to discuss the matter with Zola, who was so literary-minded and so sure of himself, always ready with an answer to everything.

In any case, according to other letters from Zola, Cézanne was haunted by the impossibility of achieving in painting what he was searching for, and that his difficulties had more to do with technique than with aesthetics. Zola felt obliged to remind him that "craftsmanship" was not everything.

This is important because it already shows what would become Cézanne's prime obsession: his incapacity. He did not doubt his vision; it was the tools for realizing it that he lacked. This lack formed part of Cézanne's basic psychological make-up, and he approached the world of art with a great deal of modesty, insisting on the fact that it was painting itself that presented the problem: he would never have become the artist he was without the desire and determination, the fervor and certainty he showed. But a new vision implies new techniques and all that Cézanne knew at the outset was that there was no pat recipe for realizing what he wanted to express in painting. "To realize"

would remain a key phrase in the Cézannian lexicon. This is crucial because it represents the first time ever in the history of art that an artist had appeared so nakedly before his destiny as a painter, and it was the first time that a painter declared so unequivocally the insufficiency of an academic preparation. The question of strategy never seems to have occurred to Cézanne; he seems to have known precisely where he was going, but it was the question of *how* to get there, of expedients, that he always came up against. Zola admonished him, "One is born a poet, one becomes a craftsman. And you who have the spark, you who possess what cannot be acquired, you complain, when all you have to do to succeed is to exercise your fingers, to become a craftsman."

Thus, the true innovator in this case was already Cézanne, and not Zola. If the question of technique had such importance, if the question of strategy could be settled by the question of expedients, it means that the two were inseparable and that art is not a question of practice. According to Zola, whoever was born a poet or an artist, whoever possessed genius, had only to practice in order to acquire technique, but according to Cézanne (and here we are anticipating in succinct terms a broader discourse that finds confirmation in his life and in his works) the difficulty lay in the gap between traditionally taught techniques and what he wanted to accomplish as a painter: to set his vision of the world on canvas, to create solely through painting technique an image that embraced his vision (in the purely optical sense of the world) and allowed him to externalize it and thus liberate himself of it. Zola could well take the French language in the state in which he found it and use it to say what had not yet been said, by changing the theme, by exposing it to the great popular legends, even if at the same time the foundations of the same language were being rocked by Baudelaire, who played with symbolic association to force the language to express more than was simply stated, and even if the ground was being prepared for Rimbaud, Lautréamont and, soon, Mallarmé. It was this very question of how-to-write and how-to-paint that gave birth to the modern culture that rapidly flowered in Europe around the time of the First World War.

Naturally, the youthful Zola and Cézanne were still far from having the slightest awareness of this important new concept and the great strides Cézanne had already made in its development. No, Cézanne was still just a young painter who desired to paint as well as the masters of the Aix museum, searching their canvases for the secret of their art, as he sought with paintbrush in hand to rediscover their techniques. Zola again wrote him, "You tell me that sometimes you throw your paintbrushes up in the air when the form does not meet with your idea of it. Why all this discouragement and impatience?" Zola distinguished between the form and the background, the technique and the content, but Cézanne's ardent pursuit was perhaps already the proof of the axiom that was to form the basis of all modern art: the form is the content, There is no content except that conveyed in and by the form. It is this equivalence between content and form, the way in which one makes up the other, reciprocally, that determines the validity of an artistic pursuit. Without ceaseless re-evaluation of its own techniques, art is nothing and so it is nothing if it does not face up to the infinite question – infinite because it has no anwer – of its own nature. Painting is not an art that makes it possible to paint what one wishes to paint, just as literature is not simply a linguistic art that makes it possible to express what one wishes to express. Art is not the means to realize the vision, it is the vision itself taking place. And if Cézanne tended to get so discouraged that Zola had to continuously try to shake him out of it, this was because he felt caught up in an impossible mission, because his passion as a painter drove him to the brink of madness.

Cézanne was a romantic young man who needed a great mission to give meaning to his life, but how could he believe that all his problems lay in his inability to apply the right brushstroke or to achieve the right form? He dramatized this because he put all of himself into each "brushstroke", and each brushstroke was so painful because it took on more significance than the simple act itself. Cézanne's shortcomings in technique were not due either to weakness or incapacity (Zola noted his having said "Technique can be acquired with work"), it was a more serious shortcoming, deeper-rooted and one that he had to overcome through his painting, an open breach inside of him between what he was and what he wished to be, a need to surpass himself and to continually test his limits, a transcendent mission that went beyond him and of which he had to be worthy. And when Cézanne threw his brushes up in the air, it was when he felt the weight of the mission too much to bear, or that it was all in vain. That there was madness in this artistic gift, he knew, as he wrote to Zola, "I have been put to nurse on illusion." Art is a path to our dreams, our imaginations, the unreal, but this is the path that Cézanne chose, the one he felt embarked upon and about which he no longer had any say. This art already made him suffer by its cruel exigence and he was no longer free to refuse its conditions; he had tried to comply with his father's wishes by studying law, but he knew right from the start that it could not last. Painting, though, was not an easy muse to win over, and she constantly denied her charms to the painter. Zola was free of self-doubt and made rather lofty claims when discussing the subject of literary or artistic creation. he was better equipped to seduce his muse of writing; she gave him what he expected of her in a continuous triumph book after book, while Cézanne seemed doomed with few exceptions to perpetual defeat and unfulfilment.

In these first letters between the two young

men, Cézanne confided to his friend his fantasies of love, another cause of disappointment; he was secretly smitten by a young woman, but one of his friends more versed in such matters beat him to the conquest. Zola entertains us with tales of Cézannian "spleen" and it comes as no surprise that for all his life Cézanne remained faithful to the poet Baudelaire, whose erotic fantasies are never without a dose of melancholy. Zola shared in this spleen only as long as he was unsuccessful in love. His was just a passing affliction, while Cézanne's was a lifelong condition. Indeed, it was a constant in Cézanne's universe – though its reflection in his paintings of nature shifted from a key of romantic dramatization to bucolic reverie with rather classical overtones. Shades of Virgil and of Lucretius are present in the works of Cézanne, as they are in Poussin.

1861: Cézanne joined his friend Zola in Paris and, according to Zola's letters to Baille, the discovery of life as a painter (which he had finally convinced his father to let him try) lent a new spirit full of promise to his work. According to the writer, the painter seemed to overcome his doubts and his paralyzing melancholy, but not much time passed before the latter wrote to his friends in Aix that he was bored in Paris, despite the Louvre, the Luxembourg and the Salon, where he had admired the "prodigious" Gustave Doré. Zola, meanwhile, wrote another letter to Baille, complaining of Cézanne's "dread of discussion". "It is impossible," he wrote, "to have a conversation with the painter. Satisfied with a few lapidary pronouncements, he refuses to discuss things in more depth." Cézanne did not like to talk of painting, he had no taste for aesthetic debate, and did not all enjoy the discussions that young painters and writers ordinarily engaged in. "Cézanne," wrote Zola, "does not admit contradiction." Then again, it was probably increasingly difficult for the painter to put up with Zola's incredible know-it-all attitude and his habit of giving advice on everything. Cézanne never discussed things, but he could say a lot with just a gesture: when he decided to return to Aix, he "smashed" Zola's portrait, probably as much in frustration over his inability to render the image he sought as over the image of a man with whom he had shared a deep friendship, but with whom he had less and less in common. (Zola, no doubt, no longer listened to him and did not understand the struggle he was engaged in. Their goals were no longer the same; the penniless writer's overwhelming hunger for social success contrasted with the painter's almost mystical commitment to his art.)

The scanty traces that remain of the successive period do not offer original or personal ideas on painting. There are but a few letters, limited to superficial chat between friends exchanging news. In a letter to Numa Coste of 1864, the main topic of discussion was Coste's imminent departure for military service. Cézanne explained to him that if he could be stationed in Paris, he would not lose all touch with painting and might even be able to take courses at he school of "bozarts", – where, Cézanne gleefully but mistakenly reported, the Institut was losing its authority. To himself he dedicated just one sentence – one that shows his capacity for self-irony in the face of discouragement: "As for me, dear friend, I am long on hair and beard but short on talent." This is little to go on if we wish to learn more about Cézanne's aesthetic ideas and interests, but the point about his hirsuit abundance does show his rejection of bougeois values and his identification with the role of the anti-conformist artist in a society that denied him a place and one which he felt he must reject in order to express himself. Cézanne, then, was one of the Parisian "bohemians"; no doubt this is not news to us, but it is interesting to see use of self-irony between friends, at the same time making it clear that the cowl does not make the friar, nor does the beard make the artist. The year before, Cézanne had only been able to exhibit at

Rue Rémy Crossroads in Auvers. 1873.
Paris, Louvre.

the Salon des Refusés, as he would do again some months after writing this letter. While he was happy to benefit by this partial solution, and was in good company (since the painters he admired had also been denied the honor of the Salon), this lack of recognition by the official institution saddened him. After all, it was not sheer wantonness that kept Cézanne on the fringes of society; his bohemian lifestyle did not partake in the romantic revolution that dreamed of the Republic and socialism and rebelled against the political and ideological power of the bourgeoisie. Cézanne was bearded but nobody recognized his talent; this laconic remark showed a good sense of humor and his modesty, but underneath it, like a pirouette at the heart of his letter, stirred the sadness of being condemned to life as a bohemian by a society that did not honor its artists.

Perhaps I have gone a bit too far in this interpretation of a minor remark taken out of context, but I would like to suggest that our knowledge of Cézanne and what we have learned about the course of his life permits us to thus decypher such information. Two years later, in a letter to M. de Nieuwerkerke, superintendent of the Beaux-Artes, Cézanne showed he was also capable of arrogance in writing on behalf of the "refusés," the painters who had been rejected by the Salon, and who no longer had their alternative Salon. When Zola published *Mon Salon*, a collection of the articles he had written in defense of the *refusés* for *L'Evénement*, dedicating the booklet's introduction to Cézanne, the latter started to enjoy a certain reputation among the dissenting artists. In a sort open dialogue, it began, "Do you know that we were revolutionaries without realizing it!" Cézanne thus carried the torch, he accepted his role as spokesman, he joined in the front-line and declared to the minister that the Salon des Refusés must be reinstated. He discourse is interesting, however, because he sustained pure individualism and spoke in terms of himself: "It suf-

fices to say to you once again that I cannot accept the illegitimate judgment of colleagues whom I myself have not commissioned to evaluate me." He stated this with a certain eloquence, but as for the other *refusés*, Cézanne limited himself to saying that if asked, they would without exception be in agreement with him... He spoke only in the first person and the letter he signed was far from being the expression of a collective movement, no less a petition. It is not surprising to learn that the minister did not even deem this personal letter from an unknown artist worthy of a response.

Five months later, Cézanne nursed this disappointment in the small village of Bennecourt on the banks of the Seine, and judging from a letter to Zola, the Parisian battle was over and forgotten. Just one thing occupied his thoughts: he was doing a painting, but for reasons that are not clear, he could only work on it for two hours a day. According to John Rewald, the artist's model was a blacksmith's son who worked all day at the forge. And even though the had "added a bit of a still life to one side of the stool," he could not continue the painting without his model. By contrast, he was working at the same time on another painting, which he judged much less important: a portrait of the inn-keeper's father-in-law that was "not turning out too badly." Thus, Cézanne seemed to place more stress on the problem of composition in the painting with the young blacksmith than on the portrait, and he was to continue to be haunted until he did his *Grandes Baigneuses* by compositions in which he was the heir of tradition, and which were later responsable for being ascribed a place in history between Delacroix and Picasso. Paradoxically, it was in his simpler canvases, the portraits and landscapes, that he gave the best of himself, he fulfilled his own vision of art. For Cézanne, there was an impossible dialetical relationship between the studio and nature, and the following autumn he clearly defined its terms, expressing with an unprecedented lucidity his problems as a painter and his aesthetic ideals. Once again, the occasion was in a letter to Zola: "But, don't you see that any painting done in the studio will never come close in value to something done *en plein air*?

"When painting outdoor scenes, the contrast of the figures against the terrain are surprising and the landscape is magnificent. I see wonderful things, and I must make up my mind once and for all to paint only *en plein air*."

This was to be Cézanne's lifelong obsession (he still had another forty or so years before him): to paint nature, to paint from life, to finally succeed in rendering his vision of nature, to capture his "color sensation." He did not discuss it more than this in his letters, always reluctant to spend more than a few vague and superficial words on his art, and was greatly embarrassed by such admirers as Emile Bernard, who would ask him to talk about his theoretical foundations. Even his correspondence with Pissarro, who had introduced him to the landscape, and whom he loved and respected, is disappointing for its banality. One paragraph, however, written in 1876 to his Pontoise friend, is an exception. In it he expressed his joy at being at L'Estaque and all of the intensity of his difficult rapport with nature: "It is like a playing card. Red roofs on a blue sea. If the weather changes for the better, perhaps I can accomplish something. As it is, I haven't yet done a thing. But there are subjects that require three or four months of work, this is possible here because the vegetation doesn't change. There are olive trees and pines that keep their foliage. The sun is so fierce that things seem to stand out in silhouette, though not in black and white but in blue, red, brown and purple. I may be mistaken but it seems to me to be the opposite of modeling." Two years later, Cézanne wrote to Zola as if in counterpoint to the above, "...I have started to perceive nature a bit late..." And, similarly in 1883, again from L'Estaque, "I have found some nice vantage points here, but this does not at all make up a subject." The landscape alone was enough to make the painting. The subject is a piece of landscape, a particular framing, as photographers say, that has given qualities that permit it to become a painting. It is unfortunate that Cézanne never did arrive at an understanding of the choice of subject, of the discrepancy between the "vantage point" and the "subject." This was one of the elements of Cézanne's recurrent painting problem... He did not doubt his talent, nor his determination, but he continued all his life to lament his block to self-realization. One senses that he never ceased to question what he chose to paint and the way in which to paint it, but neither theory nor words helped him to solve this fundamental enigma gnawing at him. Writing in 1889 to Octave Mans, who had requested some of his works for an exhibition in Brussels, he humbly explained a decision he had made after his break with the Impressionists. "Please allow me to protest your accusation of disdain in relation to my refusal to participate in painting exhibitions.

"I must say in this respect that the many studies to which I have dedicated myself have only produced negative fruits, and fearing only too justified criticism, I have resolved to work in silence, until when I feel prepared to defend with theories the fruits of my efforts."

We repeat: Cézanne was rarely satisfied with the fruits of his work, and indeed was driven by this permanent dissatisfaction. The key may lie in the definition he wrote to Joachim Gasquet in 1897: "Art is a harmony parallel to nature." This analogy was no small matter, especially when one realizes the extent to which Cézanne held nature in awe, and the gravity of the challenge he had accepted in seeking to equal that harmony. Cézanne had to conquer nature inside of himself before he could conquer it in painting – this suggests that he sought to emulate God. So this was the demiurgical task that he set before the Artist. It

104

Panorama, Auvers. 1873-75.
Chicago, The Art Institute.

was not enough to copy nature, to invest it with just any image. It was not a question of depicting nature's harmony; it was necessary to create a "parallel harmony." This was the game of high stakes that consumed Cézanne, thought he was well aware that man, lacking the Divine Grace, had to resort to other arms: "I pursue success through work," he wrote to Gasquet in 1902, and he named two other artists whom he felt his equals. "I scorn all living painters except Renoir and Monet, and I wish to achieve success through my labours." Soon after, he wrote Vollard, posing a double question that evidently implied an affirmative answer. "I have made some progress. Why so late and with so much difficulty? Is not art, in effect, a priesthood that requires the full devotion of the pure in soul?"

Emile Bernard, though not without some difficulty, managed to get him to explain himself in clearer terms, to get him to "talk painting." A single principle, "the concrete study of nature" stood in contrast to the "literary spirit." And then there is the brief declaration so frequently cited that it has become bible for the beginnings of Cubism. We quote it here in full to show, on the one hand, how incorrect this interpretation is, and on the other, how Cézanne's technical discourse is bathed in mystique: "Forgive my repeating what we discussed here: see in nature the cylinder, the sphere, the cone, putting everything in its proper perspective so that each side of an object or a plane is directed toward a central point. Lines parallel to the horizon give breadth, that is a section of nature; lines perpendicular to this horizon give depth to the whole. But nature for us men goes deeper than just the surface; hence, it is necessary to introduce a sufficient quantity of bluish tones into our luminous reverberations, shown with reds and yellows, in order to give a sensation of the air."

But how to construct things with light? How can solids be made with the immaterial? The ab-solute harmony that Cézanne sought eluded him, and his last works which seem so wonderfully airy to us were for him flawed by an insurmountable shortcoming: "I am old now, almost seventy years old. The sensations of color, which give light, are the reason for the abstractions that prevent me from either covering my canvas or continuing the delineation of objects, when their points of contact are fine and delicate; from this it results that my image or picture is incomplete."

Precisely these "incomplete" works, considered flawed by their own maker, because he never really succeeded in creating the effect he desired, are the ones that today are considered his maximum achievements for their unmistakeable mark of genius, their perfect synthesis of intellect and sensibilities in painting.

But would Cézanne really have been surprised by the judgment of posterity?

P.N. Doran's *Conversations avec Cézanne* was compiled for the most part during the artist's lifetime. It constitutes the most complete documentation of the ideas of Cézanne, apart from the Letters. This critical volume, assembled with a great deal more care than Rewald's volume of the correspondence, is indeed crucial for an understanding of Cézanne. But it would be in vain to expect to gain insight into the artist's complex relationship with painting, since outside of his painting itself it remains largely unarticulated. Doran's book is of interest primarily because the author has placed each account in its proper context, providing background information on its source, whether journalist or chronicler.

More than one art critic has dreamed the impossible dream of an interview with Cézanne, asking questions that now burn in our modern minds, but which at the end of the 19th century nobody had thought of yet. The result of this impossible interview would no doubt be surprising, but would it be any less disappointing than what we have been able to piece together with the scraps of information we have? Cézanne warned Jules Borély when they met in 1902. "Don't be surprised by my disconnected ideas. I have blank spots." Furthermore, Cézanne's ideas about painting were complicated by the fact that they were conditioned by his ideas about nature. Cézanne sought to sharpen his perception of nature in order to define what, as a painter, he could do with this nature. And the ambiguity of the relationship between the artist, nature and his painting tormented Cézanne; it was this ambiguity that he highlighted in his painting, revealing that painting is never a piece of nature, that it is not a simple image (whether set in perspective or using the Impressionist technique), but that the two things belong to separate and irreconciliable realms. Cézanne clung to these few ideas in order not to lose himself; aided by these few lifelines, he sought to invent a method that would help him to overcome his vertigo and to make progress towards his goal. Already hinted at in his Correspondence, what emerges most clearly from the Conversations is the sense of anguish he transmitted to his interlocutors when they pressed him with questions, pushing him into that impossible corner of self-explanation. He suffered greatly at this because painting, like nature, resists thought. Thus, Cézanne appeared to be foundering in a sea of unknowns; if he managed to keep his head above water, it was thanks to his painting and not to theorizing. The answer was not to be found at the end of lengthy reflection and discourse, but at the outset, since the real question was that of the artistic vision: "To paint well is a difficult thing," he confessed to Borély, "How can I get straight to nature? You see, between this tree and us there is a space, an atmosphere – agreed. But then there is this trunk, this body, so unyielding and solid." What distinguishes Cézanne from the Impressionists emerges clearly from this: for him, the object, the figure, could not be dissipated by the air and the light without losing its identity.

It was this material identity of things that he sought to paint. Neither the intellectual knowledge of things nor recourse to artistic traditions could help him in this; he had to look at the world with virgin eyes in order to grasp it. As Cézanne exclaimed, "Ah, to see with the eyes of a newborn creature!" He continued, "Today our sight is somewhat jaded, deceived by the memory of a thousand images. And the museums, the museum paintings!... The exhibitions!... We no longer perceive nature, we see paintings. To look at the work of God! This is my task."

No one has tried harder than Emile Bernard to penetrate the mysteries of Cézanne. A young intellectual painter, he was passionality devoted to Cézanne and determined to understand him, though at a certain point he had to stop pressing the artist with questions as the latter did not always answer them patiently. Thus the compendium of Cézanne's ideas turned out to be rather spare, limited to just a few remarks, phrases snatched from their context, like flowers. All the same, it can be inferred that while at first he focused on what he saw, a second phase came along in which he focused on interpretation – analysis of the subject was alone what would make it possible to proceed from the subject to the painting:

"To read nature is to see it under a veil of interpretation as successive patches of color following a law of harmony. These broad hues can then be analyzed by their modulations. To paint means to record these color sensations."

All in all, Doran's book cannot be said to offer, even in scraps, a Cézanne text. Most of the interviewers came back empty-handed. The end-product is of interest as a record of an encounter and as a portrait of a man, but not for its quotations. Emile Bernard's account amounts to a pure study of Cézanne's lifework. Maurice Denis' contribution tends in the same direction, though with less insight... Doran himself warns us about Joachim Gasquet: the scribe's recollection of his

108

Mont Sainte-Victoire. 1904.
Philadelphia, Phimadelphia Museum of Art.

Dr Gachet's House in Auvers. 1874.
Private collection

Magdalene or Grief. 1866.
Paris, Louvre.

conversations with Cézanne seem too methodical to be true. But by now we know enough about Cézanne to realize the futility of words and the inadequancy of speech. Also, since Cézanne was a painter, and passionately so – even though his youthful dream was to become a writer – it seems safe to surmise that words failed him. Moreover, he repeatedly declared and demonstrated that painting and writing were two quite separate paths. This does not mean to say that painting precludes thought, but simply that painting is another form of thought. Cézanne invited us to always look at nature and painting as if for the first time. Perhaps he even taught us to see; this would explain the great role as father of contemporary art that he played and continues to play, in abstract as well as figurative art, by way of Cubism. We shall return to this subject.

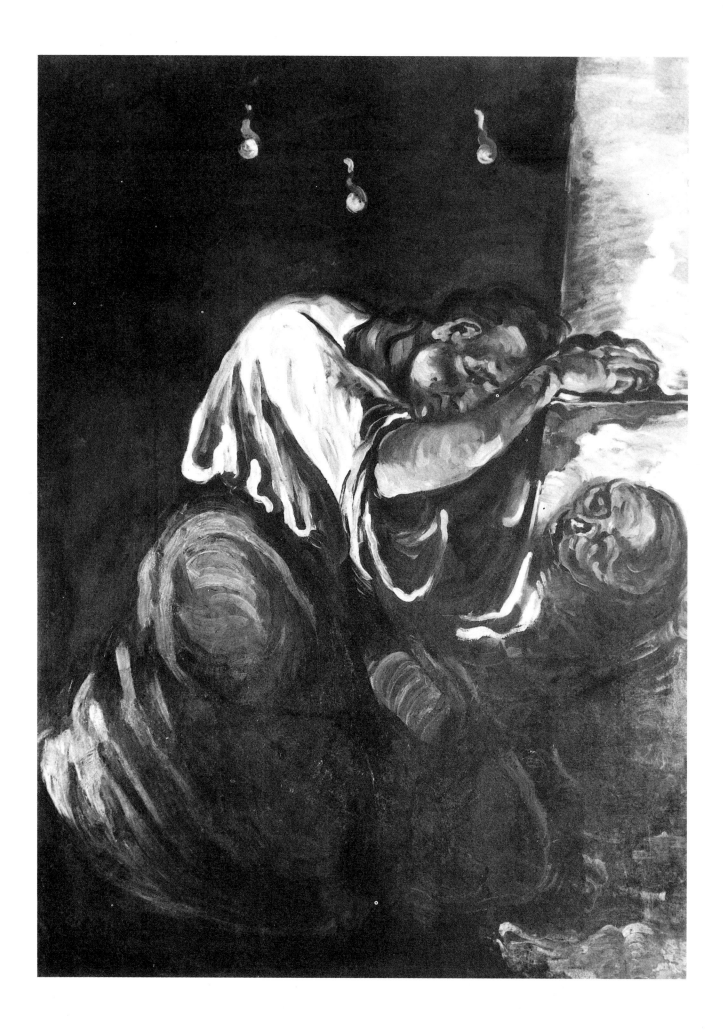

PORTRAIT OF THE ARTIST AS A HERO

Many others after Cézanne have tried to explain what he himself was never able to explain in words. It did not take long for the mystique of a man who had dedicated himself fully to painting, yet who at most only came close to his objectives of artistic creation, to capture the imagination of the public: his implacable nature, his disdain for any effort to please anybody but himself, such a firm belief in his own standards in the face of general incomprehension, underpinned by a permanent dissatisfaction with his own work – all these factor make up the Cézannian "mystique."

This modest, irrascible, solitary man, sometimes charming but more often disagreeable, showed a rare tenacity of purpose in painting; to it he gave all of himself, to it he sacrificed all in a cruel passion which offered him few fruits during his lifetime, but which finally registered a posthumous glory of surprising resonance. Now Cézanne figures as one of the founding heros of modern art, one of the great originators of contemporary painting. Cézanne has become a myth – a myth that no present-day painter can ignore, because it is there that his origins lie. For us, Cézanne started something; a momentous break with tradition took place, though he himself was no enemy of tradition. While he made a great sacrifice of himself to art, there is nothing of the romantic hero about him; he was, rather, a hardworking craftsman who pushed his professional conscientiousness to the brink of madness, and who was ill at ease with matters of ordinary existence. He was a sort of crusty recluse, awkward and well-intentioned, bent on the pursuit of an impossible dream. This is not the stuff the that heros are made of, it seems; it is not with such figures that legends are built.

Van Gogh, younger than Cézanne by just a few years, cut through the history of art like a comet. Having migrated from the mines of the Borinage towards the sun of the French Midi, he offered to the public a much more picturesque legend, with his fits of despair and madness, his sermons, his loves, his sunflowers and his amputated ear. He stole right from underneath Cézanne the leading role in the modern-day tragedy of the life of the artist in the western world, a lonely and destitute hero, armed only with his talent against the incomprehension of his contemporaries. With his striking eccentricity and his vigorous painting style, he called attention to the drama of the artist who almost against his will is invested with a mission that goes beyond him and makes him a demi-god in the eyes of posterity.

Nevertheless, Cézanne played as great a role as van Gogh in this demiurgic and sacrificial myth, even though with more discretion. His contribution was no less important than the latter's, though he did not consume himself as quickly; his passion was more contained, but it was no less moving.

As the broad public loves romantic stories and obvious images, van Gogh conquered it more rapidly and with greater ease than Cézanne, but Cézanne was the first of the two to earn the respect of the his fellow-artists. To them he proposed a new set of ideals, and he opened a door that could lead in several different directions. Despite his lack of success, his peers hailed him as a master quite early in his struggle. Both of them were suffering artists who were considered freaks before being elevated to the level of gods, and it is this shared Promethean myth that bonds them in legend.

The first version of the Cézanne myth was created by Emile Zola in his *L'Oeuvre*, a novel that took him ten years to write. Its main character is the painter Claude Lantier, and it is generally agreed that he was modeled after Cézanne. Naturally, it was not Zola's intention to write a portrait of Cézanne and some careful observers have noted that Manet and Monet may also have provided some inspiration for this character's make-up. And we must not forget the novelist's

poetic license and his imagination, which in all really must have been put to work as well in this character's formation. However, knowing the profundity of the friendship between the painter and the writer, one which was rooted in their childhood in Aix, it is not surprising to find severale references to Cézanne in Claude Lantier.

Of course, other parallels between the book and reality may be identified: the painting *Plein Air* presented by Lantier to the Salon closely resembles Manet's *Déjeuner sur l'herbe* and the main avant-garde movement of the time derived its name from Monet's painting *Impression: Rising Sun*, like the movement that Lantier led, "Plein Air." It may also be noted that starving artists were commonplace in the second half of the 19th century, ever since painting had become an individual pursuit, freed of the academies and subject to the laws of fashion and the market; in the years preceding *L'Oeuvre's* publication, some of them, like the book's hero, committed suicide.

Cézanne, unlike the book's hero, did not commit suicide, and various other details of the novel do not jibe with his life and his personality. Nevertheless, Lantier is Cézanne, there is no doubt, and he can be recognized by more than one personality trait and more than one borrowed phrase, by his mad passion for painting, his dissatisfaction with his own works, his way of brightening his palette when painting on the banks of the Seine, his intransigent egoism, his difficult relationships with women, his incredible way of letting himself be consumed by his work, his immense ambition, his desperate fits of self-doubt, his obstinate desire to plant a nude in the middle of a canvas...

Zola knew Cézanne better than any other, and had acquired most of his knowledge of painting from him. He gave to Lantier Cézanne's torment as it appeared from their correspondence (naturally, other painters have experienced torment, but not with the same intensity as Cézanne, at least not Monet or Manet). In his own way, Zola wished to write a deep psychological analysis, and he invented the character of Lantier to represent the type of artist who was a misfit in his own society. It is in fact an important document on the psychology of artistic creativity – a document fueled by his own experience as well as that of Cézanne.

Various artist-types with varying degress of talent and ideals have a role in this novel, but it does not come as a surprise that the character Lantier has a faithful friend who dates back to his schooldays: the writer Sandoz, who gives dinner parties, like Zola, and whose conversation reads closely like Zola's literary theories. Sandoz is successful by dint of hard work, but he realizes how close in spirit he is to Lantier, how he suffers from the same dissatisfaction, how art is like a disease that can only lead to the artist's undoing, even if it is also his sustenance in life.

L'Oeuvre is above all about this undoing, which goes beyond the main character's suicide. It involves the death that is etched in the heart itself of the creative process. Art can kill and art must kill. The more one puts into it, the more lethal it is. Behind every artist is a man who has died, who has renounced his existence in order to create. Cézanne was already well along on this road to death, this renouncement of life when Zola's novel was published (and, according to some, it was Zola's way of telling Cézanne that he was deluding himself, and that soon his only alternative would be suicide).

Claude Lantier hanged himself in his studio in the presence of, and following a particularly difficult session of work on, the large canvas that he had been working on for years,. One of the promising young painters of the Plein Air school, he had grown bitter and was unsuccessful at painting, in the grips of a sort of impotence that was owing less to a lack of talent than to overly ambitious aims. He had only exhibited once at the Salon, thanks to the charitable intervention of a kind soul, though

he was give a very poor position (like Cézanne). He nibbled away at his allowance, and ended up with a family of his own apparently in spite of himself, even if his wife was patient and devoted, always doing her best to help him. It is perhaps in his relationship with his wife, with women, that Lantier most closely resembles Cézanne, and starting with this glaring example, Zola demostrated great insight in his treatment of the ambiguous bonds between art, sex and death. This is the crux of *L'Oeuvre* and it is what makes the novel the first great modern epic of artistic creation.

Lantier's love for his art is too great to leave room for his wife, and Christine is well aware that painting is her great rival, the mistress that she cannot defeat. Lantier can only give himself to her when he does not succeed in giving himself to painting. He goes to her for comfort only when painting has refused to yield to him. In his painting, Lantier loves his fantasies, he loves the women that he struggles to paint, preferring the image to reality – to the point that he turns his wife into a model, nothing more than a subject for him to paint. In that wonderful last night, Christine, whose husband had not touched her for eight months, manages to win him back because his painting had abandoned him, but it is too late for Lantier to come back to life, to reality. Was he not already dead, long a condemned man because art is nothing but an illusion?

Two artists see his remains to the cemetery: the old artist Bongrand, who had recognized his talent early on and encouraged him, states plainly, "It is just as well to leave the scene than to work desperately as we do, only to produce crippled children who lack bits and pieces, the legs, the hands – children who never come alive." The writer Sandoz adds morosely, "How true. You really must abandon your pride and resign yourself to vague approximations and to cheating on life... Me, I push my books as far as I can, and despite my efforts can only feel contempt for myself

Manet. *Le Déjeuner sur l'Herbe.*
London, Courtauld Institute.

because they are incomplete and false. [...] He at least did the logical and honest thing. [...] He admitted to his failure and took his own life. [...] Since nothing can be created, since we are nothing but weak imitators, it would be all to the best to end it all right now."

Art is a dead-end street. Cézanne did not kill himself, nor did Zola. They continued to work, in spite of it all. "To work," – the novel's last words. Art is an absurd struggle, but for the artist it is the only possible way, if not to live at least not to die. *L'Oeuvre* has often been misinterpreted – starting with Cézanne, who seems to have broken off relations with Zola because of it – as a satrical portrait of Cézanne, showing him as the stereotype of the failed artist. However, a careful reading of the novel shows a thick complicity between Lantier and Sandoz, a reflection of the rapport in life between Cézanne and Zola.

Sandoz, the wiser of two, is conscious of the fact that Lantier is a part of himself, and he never professes to be superior to the painter. To the contrary, "...and now he felt as if they were going to bury his youth; it was a part of him, the best part, the one with all the illusions and the enthusiasm, that the pallbearers were lowering into the pit." Lantier, Sandoz said with admiration was very "tender-hearted," "strangled by his ideals." "No doubt, he suffered greatly. His genius was a wound that went too deep, devastating him. [...] But he was not alone in his pain... He was the victim of an era... Yes, our generation is up to its neck in romanticism, we are quite saturated with it, and though it was easy to wash ourselves in baths of violent reality, the stain persists and all the washing powders of the world will not eliminate its odor."

Zola knew very well that Cézanne would not have disagreed with the statement that "We must base ourselves on truth, on nature. This is the only possible way, and without it, madness takes hold. Fear not that the work will be flat as a result; the creator always contributes to the feeling of the work." It would be incorrect to see in Zola's Claude Lantier an exact portrait of Cézanne, no less a cold exposé of the artist's presumed "incapacity." We have seen that Sandoz felt the same "incapacity" as Cézanne – and no doubt Zola, in spite of his prolificacy, shared Sandoz feeling. He was not content with his books either, books that he knew to be no more complete than Cézanne's impossible-to-finish paintings. But Zola must have understood, perhaps simplistically, the risk that Cézanne – and he himself – ran: "Did one ever know in art where madness begins?"

The purpose of his book may have been to warn his friend and artists in general that art is a dangerous game. Cézanne was upset because he took the book too literally; the book today stands as the most generous and moving testimony of his great self-sacrifice to art, and the most aggressive declaration of the high stakes involved in the game of art. But it is Lantier's death – the end to the failings – that gives the book its empirical force, by raising it to level of myth (it is also what makes the book romantic, in spite of the naturalist claim above). And if Cézanne could not bear this vision of failure and death, it was because he saw too much of himself in Lantier, and he knew that the danger (of death or at best madness) was not simply a writer's invention. Cézanne no doubt would have preferred to have been less transparent, and to have been absolved of his role as Zola's model; it was an article on his talents as a painter that he would have preferred. Zola stressed the sacrificial side of the artisitic myth, and Cézanne may well have been touched by this, but he was jealous of his privacy – he attributed more importance to the work than to the man and he was terrified by the idea that people "might get their hooks into" him – surely he would have preferred that his friend spare him or at least focus on the quality of his work rather than on the magnitude of his sacrifice.

Cézanne, for whom "self-realization" were key words, was determined to prove himself. Lantier had failed in the demiurgic aspects of the myth, but we have seen that even according to Sandoz, this positive side of the myth is perhaps the most disappointing. The question that *L'Oeuvre* raises is about the feasibility itself of art and of creation. And Zola questioned himself as much about the vanity of his own prolixity and the illusion of his own words as about Cézanne's apparent incapacity – which, by the way, was not malicious gossip on Zola's part but a real reflection of the role that doubt played in Cézanne's work. Furthermore, Cézanne had not yet given the best of himself; he had already shown his temperament, impressed his colleagues with his genius, shown stimulating promise, but he had not yet met his own approval or that of the public and official milieu. The same goes for his youthful promise; he seemed to have re-neged on it, and it was not inconceivable that his friend began to be anxious about seeing him plunge deeper and deeper into the tunnel of failure. On the other hand, this "incapacity" was Cézanne's moving force, the expression of his ambition. At the same time, in the field of poetry, Mallarmé was placing the same high demands on himself, while for Zola (who was also a friend of Mallarmé), this represented the opposite of his dynamic and tempestuous character. Death also lay at the heart of Mallarmé's work. That Cézanne reacted badly to the image of Lantier's death is understandable, but he should not have held it against Zola for having exposed so clearly the dynamics of the Cézanne conflict.

Emile Bernard was one of the first to realize the scope of Cézanne's genius and to recognize the importance of his work. He indentified the artist's contribution to art at a time when it was just recovering from the Impressionist shock. Emile Bernard was also a painter, but one with a very intellectual and methodical approach. He was enamoured of Cézanne and was his first great critic.

His "Souvenirs sur Paul Cézanne," published by the *Mercure de France* in 1907, just a few months after the artist's death (reprinted by Doran in his *Conversations*) offers a concise, sensitive study in which the author attempts to achieve a well-balanced analysis that went far beyond just an account of a few conversations. Bernard was one of those early admirers of Cézanne's paintings in *père* Tanguy's small Montmartre shop, and in 1889, without ever having met the Aix master, he wrote the first monograph on him, generously praising his talents. He considered himself Cézanne's disciple, and would have liked to have been his successor, but it was not until 1904 that they finally met. This visit to the master lasted nearly a month. On the first day, Cézanne took him to see the "motif," the *plein air* subject he was painting having first shown him the Lauves studio. The following day, during lunch, Cézanne talked to him about Zola: "So you see that *L'Oeuvre* – in which he presumed to paint my portrait – is nothing but an appalling misrepresentation, a lie that worked entirely in his favor. [...] It was one fine day that I received *L'Oeuvre*. It was quite a blow for me."

So, twenty years later the wound was still fresh. The romantic myth of the unavailing artist's sacrifice to excessive ambition did not move him, and he still held it against his old friend for having pinned this tragic image on him. Nevertheless, the following confession, as recounted by Emile Bernard, brings us right back to Claude Lantier's obsession: "What I have failed to realize is my own vision. Perhaps one day I will succeed, but I am old and I may die before I reach this supreme height. To realize my dream! Like the Venetians." For a month, Bernard observed him as he worked on three skulls, and affirmed that each day the painting could have been considered a "satisfactory work."

The artist continually modified "the colors and the shapes." Bernard analyzed and explained in

Baigneuses. Drawing.
Private collection

udy after Delacroix's Apotheosis.
rawing. 1890-94.

depth this "brush-in-hand meditation," showing exactly where Cézanne differed from Claude Lantier. "He did not hold to an "ideal of beauty", only to that of truth. He insisted on the absolute necessity of an *optique* (perspective) and a *logique* (method). He was very strong-minded and one by he kept in check his natural gifts, and people began to think that he had become incapacitated, but he was not. Too gifted, he went too far in his reflections and into his motivations. Had he acted without so much doubt about what was best, he would not have been the Absolute that he was, he may have ceased to be an oddity, but he would have left some masterful works."

It was this pursuit of the absolute that characterized Cézanne. He developed an original method for it, applied with the precision of an alchemist: "He began with the shadow and applied a patch that he covered with a second patch, overlapping the outlines, and then a third... All these colors, acting as filters, had the effect of modeling by color the object. [...] He proceeded with a techinique similar to that which the tapestry makers of old must have used, adding successive shades of related colors until they turned into their chromatic opposites..." This makes it clear how in Cézanne's work, form and color are one – and this is not the least of his contributions to the break with traditional drawing techniques, the structure upon which all the rest of a painting hangs. Cézanne drew with paint and a paintbrush; the modulations of color made the line superfluous.

Cézanne was something like an inventor who is sure of having made a major discovery, but has not yet been able to explore its main applications. "I am too old. I have not realized my vision, and now will never realize it. I will remain a primitive on the path that I discovered." He believed in the future of painting and that art involves remaining true to nature, but Cézanne's paintings are today admired more for their beauty than for their truth. Rather, the truth that can be admired in them is and can only be Cézanne's own. And the aura of success and glory that now surrounds his work is based on his failure, which was caused by his aim of achieving the impossible; no other, let alone Cézanne himself, was ever to be a match for this aim.

Cézanne's blind belief in (if not mystification of) art contributed to his greatness, but also to his sort of madness by condemning him to eternal failure. His belief in a truth that would embrace both art and nature made him remain a traditional artist, a believer in the canons of art, who sought simply to substitute a new canon, which to him seemed true, for an old canon, which to him seemed false. But he was the first great modern artist, inasmuch as he endowed art with a nobility of purpose that until then had never been granted it: that is, until Cézanne, art had not yet rivalled nature. Never before had art been invested with such a capacity: to be capable in itself of bearing the truth, whatever the object it has undertaken to represent. Never before had the artist been charged with such a Promethean task: the conquest of a truth which owes all to him and does not spring from God. In this way, Romantic art achieved its highest expression of a religious conception of art with Cézanne, thus catching up with the great Promethean myth of poetry – the most prestigious and tragic incarnation of which was Baudelaire, who was extremely fond of Cézanne.

Bernard's portrait of Cézanne reveals a shy and kind man beneath that gruff exterior, marked also by his great anxiety. But what also comes forth is the immoderacy of man's stake in painting alongside a new notion of art and the artist – a notion that sprang from the decline of religion and the consequent direction of art's development in the 19th century. This, through the exaltation of later generations of "bohemians," is what eventually led to Pollock's passion and Rothko's suicide in a surprising line-up of dramatic lives and tragic deaths – accidental or self-willed – that constitute the subsequent chapters of a myth that started with Cézanne.

In 1921 Joachim Gasquet, the son of one of Cézanne's childhood friends, published a book he had written in 1912 and 1913 about the painter, with whom he had shared an intense friendship, despite the difference in their years, between 1896 and 1900. As Doran noted, the accuracy of what Gasquet says about Cézanne is not reliable, but Gasquet's vision of Cézanne and the image he projects through his reconstruction of conversations (that may or may not have taken place) is that of a mystic intoxicated with his sensations, where emotion fades into the infinite in an attempt to rediscover the world in its virgin state and a sensibility freed of its cultural baggage. What Cézanne offered was not so much realism as a mystical naturalism, where the artist took on the role of the high priest served by his disciples. Gasquet's Cézanne, more than Bernard's, comes from a stock of prophets; he strolls through the Louvre, celebrating Giorgione, Tintoretto, Delacroix and Courbet. And though this portrait of Cézanne is a little false, it is no less convincing, and true in its romanticized inaccuracy, in its patching together of scattered documents.

Maurice Denis tried to analyze Cézanne's teachings following their encounter shortly before the artist's death. He focused on the elements of classicism in Cézanne and how his painting corresponds to traditional ideas of great painting. He notes how difficult it is in general for anybody to say what it is that he loves – or hates – in Cézanne. "But to be precise about Cézanne – that's the hard part!" First of all, he states, "Good or bad, a work by Cézanne is always a true and proper painting." What he means by this is that it is never the subject that counts, just the style, "a particular order obtained through synthesis." Secondly, Cézanne's paintings show "an equilibrium, a harmony between the object and the subject."

Denis argues persuasively that what distinguishes Cézanne from superficial Impressionism and subjective "modern painting" is that "he worked unremittingly toward a style"; "This is the weakness of modern art that Cézanne seems to remedy, promising us a renaissance, and proposing an ideal akin to that of Venetian decadentism."

In antidote to Romanticism and naturalism, Cézanne offered "crude and rational synthesis." This ran contrary to the current of dissonance and impassioned deformation that were at the origins of Spanish painting and which El Greco introduced "into the triumphant phase of maturity of the Venetian school." Next, in reaction to the analytical vice of Impressionism, he proposed an identical synthesis intended to "create a sort of classical Impressionism." "In an era in which the artist's sensibility was almost unanimously considered the sole object of the work of art, and where improvisation [...] tended to destroy the obsolete conventions of academicism along with the requisite methods, Cézanne managed to conserve the essential role of the artist's sensibilities in his art, by substituting reflection for empiricism."

But what is striking about Cézanne's genius is that he managed this return to classicism without imitating his predecessors, discovering within himself the necessary discipline. Here Denis draw a parallel between Cézanne and Mallarmé: "Both of them scrupulously adhere to the requirements of their art without exceeding the limits," while at the same time "stripping it of all but the essential, redefining it in its purest terms." Cézanne was simply "he who paints." And inasmuch as Mallarmé is literature's equivalent of this, he is the father of a sort of symbolism which Denis defines as follows: "Every work of art is a transposition, a complement fused with feeling, a caricature, of a given sensation, or more generally, of a psychological phenomenon."

As for Cézanne's creative inadequacy, the clumsiness and imperfections that he criticized in his own work, Maurice Denis excuses them as the decadence in taste generated by the French Revolution, of which Romanticism was just the first stage. Such minor flaws are more than compensated by the "superiority of style" that allows us to glimpse a potential classical renaissance, "possibly rooted in Cézanne's method, by-product of Impressionism, in which "values" are suppressed and color contrasts are replaced by tonal contrasts." This modulation gave Cézanne the basis for a new harmony, a "delight in light" that shows his debt to Chardin. According to Denis, Cézanne's true charm, his "poetry" is indescribable; there are no words to express it. Nevertheless, it is to the critic's merit that he sought to place Cézanne in the context of art history without being blinded by the romantic myth: "He is at once the culmination of the classical tradition and the product of the great crisis of freedom and of light that renewed modern art. He is the Poussin of Impressionism. He has the refined perception of a Parisian artist, and the sumptuousness and generosity of an Italian decorator. He is as methodical as a Frenchman and as fervid as a Spaniard. He is a Chardin in decadence and at times surpasses him. There is some El Greco in him and often he has the robustness of a Veronese. But whatever he is, it comes naturally, to him and all his misgivings about his intentions, his conscientious efforts, only served to reinforce and exalt his natural gifts."

Cézanne was not assigned his place in history with due rapidity. Far from it. In his lifetime, critics did not bother with him except in mockery. A few, however, understood him better and had the early insight to know that he was shaping the art of the future. In the course of this study we have run across a few of them: Zola, Geffroy, Gasquet, Rivière, Bernard, Denis... Friends, writers, and painters who took notice and had the courage to stand up for their taste and con-

victions, when most of the critical establishment was still shrugging its shoulders about him. But this is not the place to examine such a topic, though it would be a fascinating way to study the dawn of modern art, to see how ideas slowly took hold as criticism finally opened its eyes and abandoned its prejudices.

It is surprising to see the critics' about-face following Cézanne's death when the skilful art dealer Vollard (well-assisted by the artist's son, Paul) orchestrated speculation on the works of an artist who was better loved dead than alive.

Les Maîtres de l'impressionisme, an important survey written by Camille Mauclaire in 1903, concedes but a very minor role to Cézanne, in a brief chapter entitled "Artists Working Parallel to Impressionism." Though the critic expresses some reservations in his analysis, he goes further than most of Impressionism's adulators, for whom Cézanne was nothing more than a crude dauber:

"Paul Cézanne, unknown to the public, is appreciated by a small group of connoisseurs. He is an artist who lives far away from it all in Aix-en-Provence; it is rumored that he was Zola's model for the Impressionist painter Claude Lantier, the main character in the acclaimed novel, *L'Oeuvre.* Cézanne has painted landscapes, rural scenes and still lifes. His figures are awkward and his colors ardent and clashing, but his landscapes merit attention for their solid simplicity of vision. These paintings can almost be called the work of a primitive, and they are admired by the young Impressionists because of their exclusion of all clever expedients. These works do have a certain charm in their crude simplicity and their sincerity, and Cézanne has used no more than the essential to express his ideas. The still lifes in particular are of interest for the brilliance of their colors, their clarity of tone and for the originality of certain shades similar to those of antique faïence. Cézanne is a painter without guiles; he is conscientious and intensely determined in his struggle to render what he sees and this great tenacious care has sometimes yielded results of great beauty. He must be thought of more as an old gothic craftsman rather than as a modern artist, and his work is a refreshing change from the dazzling virtuosity of so many painters."

Camille Mauclair was at least moderate in his judgment. It shows reserve but no malice. In an edition published twenty years later, he added a supplementary chapter entitled "The Reaction Against Impressionism." Following Cézanne's death, shortly after the publication of the first edition, the artist's fame expanded rapidly. Mauclair gives his personal view of this reversal of critical opinion: "The articles exposing Cézanne's genius proliferated, each writer waxing more eloquent than the next in praise that went beyond all sense of measure. In the four years since his death, Cézanne has received more posthumous approbation than Manet, Monet, Renoir and Degas in thirty years of magnificent productivity. Since the public and the critics were rather contrite about their incomprehension and their hostility towards these artists, they hastened to make amends, acclaiming Cézanne's genius, whether they understood it or not, for fear of committing a new error and wary of having to do penance for a second time."

The entire 20th century was to be marked by this guilty conscience for having misjudged the Impressionists, and the obsessive fear of repeating this error contributed in great measure to the indiscriminate glorification of a number of artists. This in fact encouraged the successive recognition of the various avant-garde movements of the century.

Mauclair's text is also of interest because it clearly shows the forces in play between Cézanne and the Impressionists, and how Cézanne profited (post-humously, of course) by the Impressionists' fame, though in life he had opposed their movement. The mechanism that resulted – dynamic yet debatable – launched all the avant-garde movements throughout the 20th century. Mauclair, re-reading himself twenty years later, found that in 1903 he had already judged Cézanne better than most critics and that he had little to add to his first version. He too considered this sudden re-evaluation of Cézanne exaggerated on the part of the younger generation, which applied new critical criteria, in part based on Cézanne's work, to free themselves of these redundant Impressionists.

Mauclair's analysis is highly releant here, as it offers us insight about the importance that Cézanne's work took on at the threshold of the 20th century. "Cézanne's work was regarded as the example of a salutary return to style and composition." He was praised for his "deep penetration of nature" in his subjects, his colors, his composition. His words and thoughts were piously gathered up in order to draw some theories from them. "Be that as it may, for some this infatuation was a simple case of bandwagonism, for others it was the almost mystical effect of a revelation, and Cézanne was soon distinguished from the Impressionists and used as an argument against them." Mauclair thus fashioned himself Impressionism's defender against Cézanne's emulators, rightly noting that the latter were trying to distinguish themselves from the Impressionists on the strength of painting theories that had not yet been fully accepted.

It is curious indeed that a painter as little inclined to literature and theory as Cézanne should have been the driving force behind this attempt to renew painting theory, one which three-quarters of a century later is far from being exhausted. But the fact remains that Cézanne's painting was sufficiently rich and raised enough questions about painting to have served as a springboard for contemporary art. Mauclair was not entirely mistaken in his opinion that Cézanne's influence

was not always beneficial, even if he was far off the mark about Matisse and Picasso: "The problems of synthesis and construction led the Cézanneans to an impasse from which the only escape for the so-called avant-gardes of painting was the spiral of veritable theoretical chaos." Today, instead, Impressionism appears to have marked the close of an epoch while Cézanne, somewhat in spite of himself, turned over a new leaf in history.

Impressionism has its charms, but we must admit that Cézanne brought us much closer to the future. Emile Bernard and Maurice Denis, among others, were quick to understand this. Bernard tried to analyze the one that Cézanne had developed into a sort of theory, but which was more of an obsession than anything else: the color sensation by which the painter allowed himself to be penetrated by nature. In this the light serves merely as a kind of catalyst. What distinguishes Cézanne from the Impressionists, says Bernard, is that he went on to analyze this sensation, seeking a new synthesis instead of simply transmitting it.

Bernard goes on at length, mainly concerned with developing his own theory. He indulges in literary flights of fancy that lack in precision. Nevertheless, he does have occasional flashes of insight, such as when he states that Cézanne had "a purely abstract, aesthetic vision of things. Where others seek to express themselves through a given subject, he is satisfied with the linear and color harmonies offered by any object, irregardless of the object itself." Or: "It is the artistic line that he offers us; he does not look at the things in themselves, but in their direct relation with painting, that is with the concrete expression of their beauty. He is contemplative, he looks with an aesthetic, not objective, eye; he expresses himself through his sensibilities, and this is to say, through his instinctive and sentimental perception of relationships and harmonies." (1904)

It is no doubt better to read Elie Faure, who already in 1910 expressed enthusiasm for Cézanne before including him among his "constructors" along with Lamarck, Michelet, Dostoyevsky and Nietzsche. With this passionate and magnificently written treatise, Elie Faure made history in aesthetic literature. His chapter on Cézanne reads like a hymn of praise. First off he sets the scene: Aix and its bourgeois inhabitants after Mass. And the silent old painter, who some called mad: "He was a wild, guileless, irascible and good-heard old man." Even at the end of his life, Cézanne had not made "amends." He was incorrigible and uncompromising.

According to Faure, the artist's "feral sensibilities" had been forced to recede in the face of the harshness of the time, of the city and of man: "The time had come to steel himself against the desperate flight of such too-childish dreams, to harden his heart against the wounds of inexhaustible human incomprehension and to open it even wider to the soothing balm of inner exploration and reprisals of hope."

Though his language is excessive, Elie Faure deserves credit for having unveiled Cézanne's force, the generous violence and crystallized romanticism that nourished his work, and that would not permit him to stop at the mere problem of aesthetics. The likes of Bernard and Denis were too intent on developing a new classicism to grasp the significance of this force, though it represents one of Cézanne's main paradoxes: his restraint is fraught with an extreme violence, his constructions are the form in which he crystallized his energy.

Elie Faure describes the climate in which Cézanne made his debuts in Paris and in the art world: "Romantic spiritualism was suddenly giving way to experimental materialism," and this was a contradiction that always played a great role in Cézanne's life and work. "The artist was no longer subject to literary contraints. It was the scientific constraint that was starting to take hold," and Cézanne – in spite of his passion for literature – stripped his work of all narrative. Though the scientific did not interest him, his work beliees a certain "experimental materialism" applied to the art of painting. And rather than having substituted reflection for empiricism, as Denis said, Cézanne focused his reflection on his own experience. Cézanne's was an experimental painting, free of narrative and of theory, adventurous and revealing. He did not give in to the temptations of science – to seek the recipes of painting in the optical laws set forth by Chevreuil – an illusion that the Impressionists had entertained. Indeed, this made him feel even more acutely the need to assure himself of fundamentals of art which were solidly anchored in tradition.

Whereas his new friends had, with much fuss, opened the window to let in the perfumed air of the countryside and natural light, he perceived that his older friends had long stood silently at this window observing the confused intersecting of lines, the complex dance of light and the movement of shadows and of men, seeking in them particular accents and prevailing orientations whose repetition and cyclical nature could take on the force of law. Cézanne set about unveiling a secret of the world, but without resorting to old formulas, and, rather, stripping tradition of the preconceived ideas that had stood between the artists and their sensibilities. Cézanne was also the first great individualist in the history of painting: "From within him stirred such profound and confused desires that the ambient sounds prevented him from hearing them. Solitude alone could give him counsel..."

Elie Faure, with his extraordinary sense of formula put his finger on one of the keys to Cézanne – the one that was to open the door to Cubism and beyond to all abstract art. "Since he fled the anecdotal in art, anecdote fled his life." Faure's portrait of Cézanne is one of the handsomest and the most precise because he manages to capture the artist's greatness behind the guise of an irascible old man. It would be a pleasure to quote longer passages, following with Elie Faure the course of this life, which he recounts with his characteristic passion, if we did not have to dig deeper to discover what he understood of the importance of Cézanne's work. His description is well worth remembering: "This is a primitive exploration of the overall and enduring architecture of the earth, a piece of it transferred with its deepest foundation strata to the space of a painting."

At this point in our study, we are well-versed on the painter's relationship with nature ard must turn our attention to broader view of his contribution to art. Cézanne was tireless in his search of a truth and the pictorial form of this truth; his approach was personal, "primitive," and he relied only on his own vision, using a method that he perpetually fine-tuned on a purely empirical basis, diverging from the canons only when his personal experience demanded it, without seeking to apply scientific principles.

Because Elie Faure's lyricism is a far cry from the contemporary critical vernacular, one may misjudge its content and ridicule his boldly compressed turns of phrase, but he does offer some powerful insights that get to the heart of the time and the place, the historical and social contexts. "It was thanks to Cézanne that the much-needed renaissance of the Southern aesthetic" – desired by Ingres (whom Cézanne never forgave for his narrow scope) and sketched out by Daumier (whom he venerated) with such virile accents, – "took place at the close of the century. One day there shall be unity, and the railways that transport in hours men from the land of the beech trees to that of the olive tress, and the words that fly in seconds from the shores of fire to the fields of ice, and all the thoughts and desires from all corners of the world, will intermingle and clash, enriching one another, creating one minute of joy for us, a single and multi-faceted soul where Aeschylus and Shakespeare meet."

This dialectic between the north and south plays an important role in the development of European culture, especially in France, where the language itself has conserved the traces of a borderline dividing the country in two. Until the 20th century French painting was usually aligned with either with Flemish or Italian trends. Then it became Parisian-based because that was the center of political and cultural power (the Ile de France triumphed with Impressionism). And if it strayed away at all it was only to follow the course of the Seine, or to make a quick get-away to the Channel coast, which was a vacation outpost of Paris. Cézanne was from the South and despite some forays to Paris, he remained a Southerner. He was also the first painter of his province to have acquired fame at the national, and later international, levels. By birthright and experience, but also – and more importantly – by right of the subjects he painted, he was a native of the French Midi. Though his Provence was landlocked rather than seafaring, Cézanne showed a mediterranean concept of the earth, haunted by the likes of Virgil and Lucretius: "There was not a single loose link in the fabric of things, not a breach through which an element of dissociation from the land could creep in. It all held together in a solid block."

It would be mistaken to believe that Elie Faure let himself be carried away by literary effects. After having attempted to penetrate to Cézanne's very roots, to understand the artist's place in the world, and hence the impulses behind his work, he did not neglect to emphasize the effect of being a painter on Cézanne's personality. "He was a painter. Nothing inerested him except formal and chromatic combinations created by light and shadow on objects..."

Thus Cézanne was a painter. That is to say, a painter first and foremost, and more so than any-one who had come before him. We must interpret Faure's point in this way: that Cézanne was the very essence of painting itself. And in some sense the first painter. It is not surprising, then, to read the opening of Roger Fry's analysis, *Cézanne. A Study of His Development*. "Those artists among us whose formation took place before the war recognize Cézanne as their tribal deity, and their totem." The Moses of a dynasty. The Moses of contemporary painting. Fry attempts to identify what is great and original about Cézanne and what makes him run up against impossibility: "To describe Cézanne 's work, I find myself, like a mediaeval mystic, before the divine reality, reduced to negative terms. I have to say first what it is not." Fry attempts to stalk the secret of Cézanne on the road that lies between his first and last works. He starts with those romantic, pasty, Baudelairian first works, inspired by Delacroix and Manet. They are clumsy and naive, but already show a special sense of color. "The extreme clarity and luminosity of these sober colors... show how essentially a painter Cézanne was by nature."

According to Fry, in an epoque of painting that Cézanne himself described as "spineless," the artist was torn by contradictions; he gave into temptations that were contrary to his nature. This went on until Pissaro taught him respect of nature and the technique of the juxtaposition of colors. From them Cézanne proceeded toward increasing lightness and transparency: "...as we advance in the chronological sequence of his works, we find his materials become less and *pastose*, his touches more and more liquid and trasparent, more like watercolor." At the same time, he worked ceaselessly on his compositions. The portrait of Geffroy and the *Cardplayers* represent "...the triumph of that pictorial probity of modern art... for Cézanne's purely plastic expression reaches the depths of imaginative life." Such statements unfortunately lack explanation, and despite the accuracy of Fry's study, the author did not succeed in justifying his passion.

Meyer Shapiro goes further in his analysis of Cézanne's style, giving us a clear grasp of the artist's historical contribution. "The strokes of high-keyed color which in the Impressionist paintings dissolved objects into atmosphere and sunlight, forming a crust of twinkling points, Cézanne applied to the building of solid forms. He loosened the perspective system of traditional art and gave to the space of the image the aspect of a world created free-hand and put together piecemeal from successive perception, rather than offered complete to the eye in one coordinating glance as in the ready-made geometrical perspective of Renaissance art." But Shapiro attributes the birth of "pure painting" to Manet, inasmuch as the term "meant the dedication to the visual as a complete world grasped directly as a structure of tones without intervention of ideas or feelings about the represented objects; the objects are seen but not interpreted."

According to him, Cézanne did not adhere to this principle: "The object has for him the same indispensable role that the devotion to the human body had for the Greeks in creating their classic sculpture."

Indeed, while Impressionism decomposed the object, the "motif," culminating in Monet's great water and plant themes, Cézanne did his best to celebrate the object, whether an apple or a mountain, giving it volume and weight. In this way, he was more of a painter than the others; not satisfied with simply capturing the color sensation of the object, he sought to reconstruct it in paint. "Cézanne's accomplishment has a unique importance for our thinking about art. His work is living proof that a painter can achieve a profound expression by giving form to his perceptions of the work around him without recourse to a guiding religion or myth or any explicit social aims." At the threshold of the 20th century, Cézanne proved

that painting is a purely individual and personal experience – and not just because of his circumstances as the lone artist, but also in his way of painting. It remains to discover what gives Cézanne his universal impact, for not even Shapiro was able to solve this enigma of the simple but mysterious lifework of the artist.

We owe the most accurate analysis of Cézanne's quest and the deepest understanding of his lifework to Pierre Francastel. He places it within the historical context of Europe, which at the start of the 19th century was still dominated by a concept of space that had been developed in the Renaissance, in breaking with the projective and egocentric vision of the world that was typical of the Middle Ages. Since the medieval artist conceived of the world as the materialization of God's thought, "he did not bother with problems of proportion and of placement of things in relation to one another."

According to Francastel, "the Renaissance undertook to render the world concrete, no longer with values and concepts, but with figures." His broad historical and sociological perspective invites us to go beyond the emotion that our contemplation of a work of art arouses in us, and the poetic reverie it inspires in us. All art is a sum total of signs that take on a meaning in function of the artistic idiom's state of development at the moment in which it is produced. Focusing in particular on the artistic representation of space, Francastel shows now this is a basic datum of painting, that it is the element in which the ideological imports tied up with a given moment in history and the society's perception of itself are most evident. Thus, with the Renaissance arose the idea that the world is no longer "a concrete representation of God's ideas," but a "society in itself, a natural system."

Space, both psychologists and mathematicians inform us, is all in the mind: "The idea of a natural, immutable space, which the arts continue to

The Jas de Bouffan.
Oslo, National Gallery.

Père Lacroix's House. 1873.
Washington, National Gallery.

convey with more or less fidelity, is in contrast to all that we know about perceptive and mental structures, as well as to all that the critical examination of works of art tells us." The Renaissance space was born of a new concept of the world, in relation to the expanding role of science and "a new state of mathematical knowlege" that made it possible to perceive the world in a new way, and also produced the means to act on this world: perspective is the most typical expression of this, inasmuch as it is the sign of a new way to represent the world at the same time in which it is the tool for a new way to construct the world in and by architecture. "The new space is a mix of geometric and symbolic representation where technological know-how is at the service of all."

We know today that perspective is not true to life. It is an illusion: "Of course, all men can be led to see how the two lines of a road's edge seem to meet at the distant horizon [...] but it is important to note that this is a perception of a given sensation within a geometric – that is to say, intellectual – context that assumes some acquired knowledge, Moreover, men can just as well be led to see overlapping perspectives, for example, as obvious and tangible reality, or a series of juxtaposed images in the Egyptian style, given another system of integrating their sensation into a particular individual and social construct."

Since scientific, geographic and plastic spaces change according to society and its stage of development, they can be neither penetrated nor left suddenly. The Renaissance space, which can be roughly described as classical, was born in the 15th century following a lengthy period of gestation. It lasted for more than four centuries before being called into question by this. Europe-wide twinge of conscience that revolutionized the European culture's lines of force, exploding at the same time as the French Revolution, developing into that vast current of Romanticism which then determined our contemporary culture. It all began

in the 18th century with "the great subject debate" that raged in painting for an entire century before the Impressionists defined the contemporary subjects in a "style of painting that was at once poetic and realistic." But the issue of the subject eclipsed to a certain extent questions of a plastic nature and Romanticism was "careful not to rock the massive foundations of the plastic representation of space."

The Impressionists challenged this order. First, by offering "a new way of depicting space, but not in relation to a new way of seeing." A new "use of color in representation" was at first placed on the Renaissance framework, but it did not stop there. Manet, Degas, Monet and Renoir gradually began to show a different space, "limitless and measureless and simultaneously intimate and decorative," in which the figures entered into a new kind of relation with the others, not geometric (set in perspective). They based themselves on a view of the world in close-up, that is, an "inquisitive view which was no longer satisfied with generalized sensation." As we have seen, Cézanne fully benefited by their experience, but had no peace until he had gone beyond it, by integrating it into a system of eternal plastic values.

At this point Francastel lingers on the evolution of Cézanne's work, and the contradiction that haunted the artist: an almost religious respect of "tradition" as embodied in Poussin versus a spirit of discovery that made him into a valiant revolutionary. It is not as simple as that: Cézanne, in truth, is not a comforting figure," and it would be facile to dismiss him as having the sensuality of the Impressionists enriched by Romanticism. Similarly, Cézanne's work cannot simply be hailed as the triumph of Classicism over Romanticism – no more than as a fictitious reconciliation of opposites. Cézanne marked the dawn of an era, rather than the close of an epoch. He opened a door rather than closing it.

His originality did not lie in his different way of

seeing familiar objects, nor in his application of acute sensations to earlier technical schemes. It had to do with his interest in novel aspects of optical perception. Starting with an incredible feeling for nature such as what the Impressionists described, through a rigorous selection process he isolated a number of meaningful fragments lacking in classical value. He created a world that was at once fragmentary and organically whole, working on the basis of a "few fundamental principles and following only his certainty of a specific truth."

In this way the Cézannian revolution took place, in an open space where the artist was free to work according to his own personal requirements. Cézanne discovered the strong bonds linking the lines of perspective to one another and holding them firmly in place: "The aim of painting according to Cézanne was the discovery of fragments of nature that could express the painter's interest in the world. The artist's place in society no longer counted, rather it was his position in the universe. [...] The humble apple may elude the artist, while the mountain is open and yielding to his touch."

What Cézanne has come to represent to us a century later is no longer the artist portrayed in *L'Oeuvre*, who died before achieving his vision. He has become a hero, the artist who opened a new world in painting, which we are just beginning now to explore.

Whoever writes about painters must eventually run up against his own inadequancy, since in painting the essential defies words; what is expressed visually cannot and need not be reduced to the word. For whatever reason. Painting is always a thought that has not been verbally expressed and that can only be expressed in images. Critics later try to put it in words, to make it conform to their order of ideas, and often, to reduce it to a few formulas. However, we cannot avoid the questions that painting asks us, the reflection that

a work stimulates in us. Is it right, then, in respect of painting, to remain mute in silent reverence before it? To be content with the feelings it rouses in us? It is a tempting proposition. But given the confusion of tastes, the rivalry of trends, the web of illusions that delights our eye, how can we avoid resorting to words and contemplation? How can we quell the urge to think about a given painting, to compare it to other paintings we have seen, and to draw from this its maximum significance?

What role does meaning play in Cézanne's work? To what extent does this object – one or another of his canvases – have a meaning? Space does not permit us to examine this fascinating question in great depth, and we must be satisfied with a few brief observations of a psychological or aesthetic nature that will help us to understand Cézanne as a man and as a painter. If we have dwelled on the biographical details of his life, it was because we felt that it would shed light on the creative process, on the forces that make up the fabric of an artist's existence. We have indulged in a few anecdotes, only because the public is interested in knowing about the man behind the artist. Rightly so, for while an artist's merit lies in his work, one can understand his work only by learning more about its genesis – that is, about the man who gave expression to it, who has attempted to give a meaning to his life through it.

Cézanne offers us an extraordinary example of one man's determination in artistic pursuits. Painting wreaked havoc in his life, conditioning his dreams and desires. He worked with extreme conviction, though always asking himself the same question, the one that no artist can avoid: to what purpose? Nevertheless, Cézanne would never have amounted to anything without his painting; he was just a modest man, a little on the uncivilized side, whose only concerns (barring painting) would have been the ordinary ones of anybody else living in his time. And we cannot help but wonder how such an insignificant little

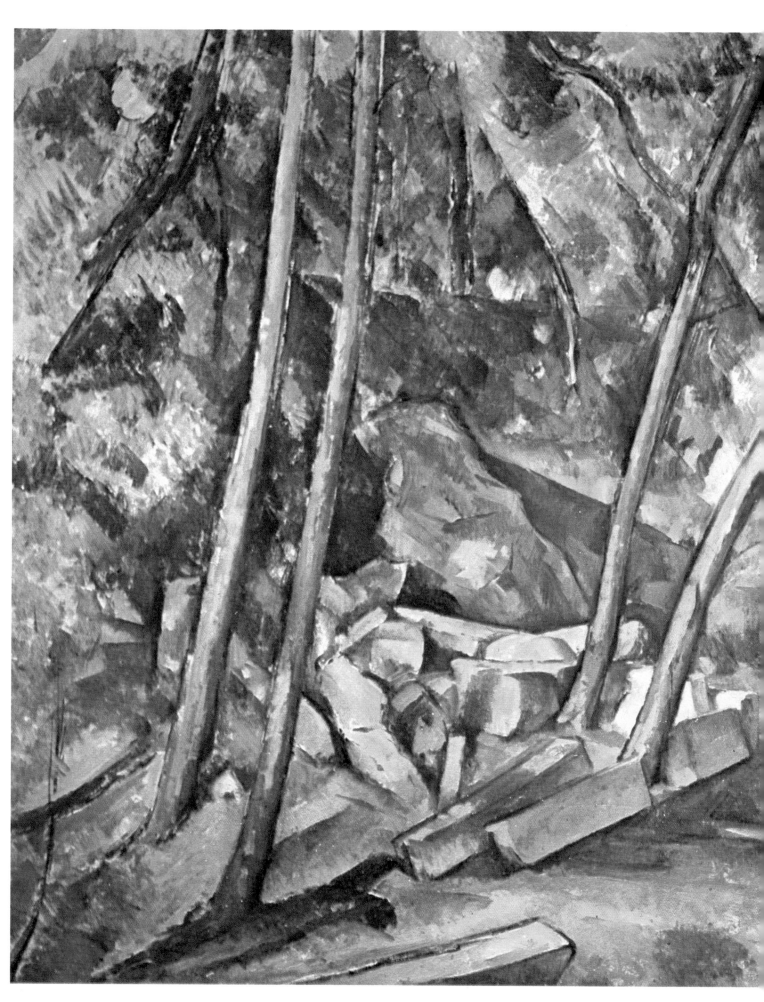

Grinding Wheel in the Forest of the Château Noir.
Philadelphia, Philadelphia Museum of Art, Tyson Collection.

man, who stripped of his painting would have shown no trace of genius, could have produced works that have dominated our century.

Unfortunately, the sketchiness of the studies dedicated to Cézanne and the weakness of the theories developed in relation to his work have prevented us from explaining more fully the greatness of the man's work and its influence. Art criticism is still a new science, but even so, it is surprising how inadequate and superficial the literature on Cézanne is, to the point that a study of his life is far more revealing that one of his works.

It is not aim here to rectify this situation. It would be a long and exacting job. Therefore, we have stopped at a few broad ideas whose only purpose was to attempt a new and all-embracing summary of the Cézanne phenomenon, which is as interesting from a psychological as from an aesthetic or art historical point of view. The incredible success of the "Final Years" exhibition in the United States and France suggests that this could be a sociological phenomenon as well. It may be that today Cézanne, fixed in the mythical role as the suffering artist and as the legendary father of Cubism, is the crystallizzation of a current taste that, following the Impressionist vogue, has swept both sides of the Atlantic.

As for the myth of the suffering artist, we have seen that he brought it on himself, apart from an unfortunate relationship with his father (all very relative) which he might have resolved had he not preferred to accept some material comfort in exchange. A modern-day psychoanalyst may have observations to make on the paternal influence in Cézanne's life – we have seen how it was not a minor factor in his painting, but it is not within our competence to discuss it in more depth. Marcelin Pleynet ventures further in this respect, with a bold style of inquiry that focuses more on the mystery of artistic creation than on evaluation of the work itself.

In truth, the myth of the suffering artist is hackneyed in Europe, after a century of use. The momentary incomprehension of the public is no reason to suffer. Whoever tries to say something that has never been said before should not be dismayed by the few receptive ears he finds. It takes time, and fame is more often than not posthumous. Furthermore, Cézanne never lacked in admirers and though they were rare, perhaps they followed him more closely than a broad public would have. The suffering artist was entirely his own doing, because he had made the decision to sacrifice himself to art. He suffered at his own hands for this dream, to which he dedicated himself and which permitted him to escape a reality to which for one reason or another he could not adjust himself. That is another story... And, after all, Cézanne had to cede the first place among suffering artist to van Gogh, a more tragic hero for lovers of romance.

And as for Cézanne as the father of Cubism: this theory hangs on a single brief, rather ill-fated and vague statement of his about a few geometric shapes – the cylinder, the sphere, and the cone – that, besides, was made in reference to a conception of space promoted by the Renaissance. This is made clear in the rest of the statment – so readily overlooked by those seeking to prove their point – which reads, "putting everything in its proper perspective..."

His only original contribution to theory, then, was to complement the canons of perspective with another canon which grew out of the Impressionist experience, but which Cézanne expressed in a personal way, in all of his works: "to introduce a sufficient quantity of bluish tones into our luminous reverberations, shown with reds and yellows, in order to give a sensation of the air."

Going on this slim evidence of theory, one could reduce Cézanne to this formula: perspective + air. But we have subscribed to Pierre Francastel's analysis, according to which Cézanne opened the space in painting, he freed it of the static structure imposed by the canons of perspective. Furthermore, even accepting that Cubism (at least the early examples, in Braque's and Picasso's first experiments) was an offshoot of Cézanne's works, it should be pointed out that it relied less on geometrical shapes – which long before Cézanne had been the domain of art, and to which Cézanne was not even particularly attached, whatever he said (and this geometric whim was no doubt simply an affirmation of his respect for the classical tradition, timeless structures and his taste for the solid) – than on the flattening of space.

Cubism broke more definitively with the canons of perspective than Cézanne ever did. And though the latter has finally been accepted by the broad public, the first Cubist works can still be shocking to a lot of people. This is because the technique of multiple perspectives – which already in a number of Cézanne's paintings creates a feeling of disequilibrium, in Cubism is pushed to an extreme, suppressing the background and merging the subject and its setting in a kaleidoscopic whirl of multi-faceted forms. Cubism barged in through the door that Cézanne had left open, uniting different perspectives of the subject on the single plane of the canvas, but it overlooked the companion contribution that Cézanne made to art: the depiction of the depth, the substance of air through blue tones, which he perfected in his last paintings of Mont Sainte-Victoire.

While Cézanne substituted one form of depth for another, Cubism ended up by seeing only a single plane. Similarly, it no longer examined nature, but instead favored the still life over the lively outdoor scenes exalted by the Impressionists. This was its limitation. Braque and Picasso soon abandoned their initial severity only to be ensnared in the mesh of a renewed academicism, though all the while heeding Cézanne's lesson of spatial freedom. Of course, it is inconceivable to dismiss Cubism as merely a development of Cézanne's work, since many other factors must be taken into account. It was the dawn of a new century. Nevertheless, it was not by chance that painting henceforth developed along very divergent lines, among which abstract art was not the least important (once the need for perspective had been disproven and pictorial space had been freed, the question of subject resurfaced in a radical way).

In the history of European painting, Cézanne occupies a key position betwen Impressionism and Cubism, but it is reductive to limit his role to having ensured the transition between these two movements and to having eluded the trends of his epoque, while Impressionism and Cubism, like all avant-garde movements, soon got mired in an academicism that enjoyed only a fleeting moment of popularity. To see Cézanne as the culmination of Impressionism or the beginning of Cubism is too simplistic a view of historical evolution, too linear to be true. In dwelling on a few of Cézanne's ambiguities, my purpose was also in part to complicate this simplistic vision, and to promote the idea that what is at stake in art is more than just a series of passing movements, more than the history of the discovery of a few formulas that linked together would allow art to enhance its powers – the study of art history is not the study of technological know-how.

Cézanne invites us to consider this unsurmountable paradox: his revolutionary work prepared the way for contemporary art, and yet it eludes history. But is it not fitting that revolutionary contemporary painting be based on such a paradox? Is it not thanks to such ambiguity that modern art has been able to evolve in all directions without ever making progress?

Cézanne pushed the logic of Impressionism to the point of its own destruction: he turned their technique of chromatic decomposition into a technique of luminous unification. In the solitude

of an apparently isolated experience in the course of the century he performed this sleight of hand, regardless of any historical logic and though he was consumed by his private obsession; he would find no solution to his existence except in painting. He dealt a blow to painting from which it never recovered: no doubt Picasso drew the most profit from this blow, above and beyond the fleeting and slightly over-rated experience of Cubism.

In some ways and in spite of himself, Cézanne was a great revolutionary, not because he sought revolution but because his life, before anyone else's, prepared the ground for its explosion. He realized that he had to rely exclusively on his own experience rather than on that of his teachers or of his culture. He compared himself to Moses marching endlessly towards a Promised Land which he would never reach. He was indifferent to disciples, and indeed perceived those who paid him homage as thiefs ready to strip him of his secrets. But the metaphor he used to describe his impossible undertaking today has taken on a meaning that he certainly never considered: though Moses never reached the Promised Land, he had glimpsed it. Thanks to his enlightened leadership, others coming after him were able to arrive there. In this way Cézanne's sacrifice of himself to painting was not in vain: not only did he leave us these wonderful works, but he made it possible for painters who followed him to know the Promised Land of painting, where painting is freed of the laws of optics. In this land of free painting, others could sow seeds that later came to fruit – even if few can claim to match the lucid charm of Cézanne's works.

Another paradox: today, Cézanne figures as the man who freed painting, but how can we forget how great his struggle was to cast off the shackles of tradition? He was the living proof that in art, freedom is nothing if it is not hard-earned. And nothing in Cézanne is gratuitous. His struggle as a painter was not simply that of freeing pictorial spaces, and his intention was not simply to tear down the citadel of perspective; our seasoned eyes risk to forget the shock that he created in his time, and it is difficult for us to really see the breakthrough that his art represented – though the value of this new art does not lie only in its novelty. Since then, we have seen many "differences," novelties, originalities.

What constitutes the novelty of Cézanne's art is first of all, the meaning that Cézanne's experience itself gives to it – his struggle with the angel of painting, which sums up practically his entire life, and which Zola portrayed accurately. It is from Cézanne's uncompromising destiny as a painter that his work takes its meaning, its testimonial value, its alchemical quality: it is a crystallization of human experience to which we cannot remain indifferent. But if we must halt at this point of view, we would remain prisoners of a dramatic vision of art that does not explain why others have burned with the passion of painting, but have not produced works that we could include in our stock of artistic treasures. The profundity of Cézanne's experience gives a human quality to his works that touches us and stimulates an emotive reaction; this is what conquered the huge public that today reveres him. This is what lets his works be expressive without the need for critical analysis.

But this is not enough. Though it is an essential guarantee of the quality of his work, it can be deceptive. At the very least it risks wearing thin, since nothing deteriorates as quickly as an emotion when there is nothing to renew it. But Cézanne's work retains the power of its meaning, as if it always has an answer for whomever questions it. The particular place it occupies in the history of painting – as the source of contemporary art – gives it a seminal value that cannot be overlooked. It acquired its true meaning only as time passed, and this is why it was not immediately accepted; successive generations gave it its meaning and continue to do so as they seek to penetrate its secrets and achieve the maximum insight into its meaning.

Great works of art never lose their power over us, as they are rooted in the deepest realms of man's imagination while simultaneously calling into question his language. By definition, all great work remains open to interpretation, which is renewed by each fresh gaze that rests on it. Its interpretation remains outside of history because it takes place in the heart of the individual, while at the same time it is a turning point in history because it lies at the heart of an epoch's re-examination of its own means of expression. Cézanne's Oeuvre is for us today one of the richest that exists. The essence of this work lies in its incomplete state in the eyes of the artist; for this very reason it stays alive, it lends itself to the game of renewal and to an ever-widening circle of interpretations.

Maurice Merleau-Ponty wrote about Cézanne that "Because he delves into the depths of the mute and solitary experience that lies at the foundations of culture and the exchange of ideas, the artist launched his work as a lone man launched the first word, not knowing whether it would be more than a cry, or if it would be able to free itself from the flux of an individual life, where it was born." This is the wonder of Cézanne, and what makes him in a certain sense the first painter: he did not do in painting what had been done before him and what continued to be done after him. He spent his life in quest of a painting that eluded him, like a Promised Land of art, where all can be said, and perfectly. Cézanne turned back to the origins of painting , inviting us to follow him, to this instant in which the canvas is white, when the first brushstroke or the first color is to be applied. Nothing is taken for granted in this birth of painting – nothing but a man at large in the world, immersed in an infinity of lines and color. Starting with Cézanne, painting entered into a state of eternal renewal, and in this sense Cézanne can be said to have closed the door on painting history just as he was opening it on painting. For today and ever after, we are present at the birth of painting.

1839	Paul Cézanne is born on January 19 in Aix-en-Provence, son of Louis-Auguste, milliner and later banker.
1852-1898	He meets Emile Zola at school. It is the dawn of a friendship that will have great importance in both of their lives.
1858	Passes his Baccalauréat.
1859-1860	Law studies and art classes. Paints four large panels in the style of Ingres for his father's home.
1861	Paris. Meets Pissarro. Fails the entrance examinations to the School of Fine Arts. Return to Aix to work in his father's bank.
1862	Returns to Paris and meets most of the future Impressionists.
1863	Exhibits at the Salon des Refusés. In the years that follow he divides himself between Aix and Paris, discovers Wagner and is regularly rejected by the official Salon.
1866	Zola publicly defends Cézanne's painting.

1868	He meets Hortense Fiquet who was to be his companion and later his wife.
1870	Manages to avoid military service, remaining in the Midi to paint.
1872	Paul Cézanne is born, son of the artist and Hortense Fiquet, who are not yet married. The painter kept his son's existence a secret from his family at length. He settles at Anvers-sur-Oise guest of doctor Gachet, who was later to offer his hospitality to van Gogh.
1874	Participates in the Impressionist first exhibition, showing *La Maison du Pendu* and *A Modern Olympia*.
1877	Exhibits for the last time with the Impressionists.
1878	Spends the year in the Midi with Hortense and young Paul. Works intensely with Pissarro.
1882	Exhibits at the Salon
1883	Stays in the Midi for the year and sees much of the Marseillese painter Monticelli.

1884	Gains recognition in Paris among the young artists who discover some of his works at *père* Tanguy's shop in Montmartre.
1885	His romantic involvement with a servant hired by the Cézanne family causes a local scandal.
1886	Zola publishes *L'Oeuvre* and Cézanne breaks with him. He marries Hortense. Inherits his share of the family estate.
1889	*La Maison du Pendu* is shown at the Exposition Universelle.
1890	Exhibits three works in Brussels. Goes on long tour of Switzerland with his wife and son.
1891	Declines to exhibit at the Salon des Indépendents. A survey of young painters is published by the journal *L'Echo de Paris* which confirms Cézanne's influence. Becomes devoutly Catholic.
1894	Caillebotte bequeaths his collection to the State, including several works by Cézanne. Some of these are accepted for the Luxembourg Museum collection.
1895	First solo exhibition, sponsored by Vollard who from now on would be his dealer.

1897	His mother's death deeply grieves him.
1898	Vollard organizes another exhibition.
1899	Exhibits at the Salon des Indépendents. Settles definitively in Aix.
1900	He is well-represented at the great exhibition organized for the Centennial.
1902	Zola's death disturbs him despite their falling-out.
1904	Long converstions with Emile Bernard. An entire room (30 paintings and 2 drawing) is dedicated to him at the Salon d'automne.
1905	A survey conducted by the *Mercure de France* reveals that his influence on young painters is growing steadily. Admirers flock to pay him homage.
1906	October 22. Paul Cézanne dies of complications resulting from a chill he had taken some days earlier while caught in a rainstorm as he painted.

Cézanne — *Correspondance*, with foreword by John Rewald (Grasset, Paris 1978).
Conversations avec Cézanne, critical edition with foreword by P.M. Doran (Macula, Paris 1978).

Emile Zola — *L'Oeuvre*, with foreword by Antoinette Ehrard (Garnier-Flammarion, Paris 1974).

Roger Fry — "Le Développement de Cézanne" (in *L'Amour del'Art*, Paris, Dec. 1926).

Lionello Venturi — *Cézanne, son art, son oeuvre* (Paul Rosenberg, Paris 1936).

Henri Perruchot — *La Vie de Cézanne* (Hachette, Paris 1956).

Camille Mauclair — *Les maîtres de l'Impressionnisme* (librairie Ollendorf, Paris 1924).

Maurice Meleau-Ponty — *Sens et non-sens* (Nagel, Paris 1948).

Pierre Francastel — *Peinture et société* (Denoël, Paris 1977).
Cézanne, les dernières années (1895-1906), exhibition catalogue, Grand Palais (Paris 1978).

Marcelin Pleynet — "Cézanne sous l'oeil paternel" (in *Documents sur*, n° 4-5, Paris, June 1979).